MW00610801

Odds Are, You're Going to Be Exalted

Odds Are, You're Going to Be Exalted

Alonzo L. Gaskill

Salt Lake City, Utah

Visit us at DeseretBook.com

Library of Congress Cataloging-in-Publication Data

Gaskill, Alonzo L.
Odds are, you're going to be exalted : evidence that the plan of salvation works / by Alonzo L. Gaskill.
p. cm.
Includes bibliographical references (p.) and index.
ISBN 978-1-59038-918-8 (hardbound : alk. paper)
1. Salvation—Mormon Church. 2. Church of Jesus Christ of Latter-day Saints—Doctrines. 3. Mormon Church—Doctrines. I. Title.
BX8643.S25G37 2008
234—dc22 2008005298

Printed in the United States of America
Worzalla, Stevens Point, WI

10 9 8 7 6 5 4

For my children—
That they might have hope

Contents

CONTENTS

ACKNOWLEDGMENTS

I acknowledge the invaluable contributions of several individuals who took time out of their busy schedules to read drafts of this book and offer suggestions that have greatly improved the manuscript, namely, Vance R. Bohman, Matthew B. Christensen, Lori K. Gaskill, Richard G. Moore, Kenneth N. Shaw, Daniel R. Winder, and Eric L. Wing.

I also express my gratitude to the editors and staff at Deseret Book for their ever impressive work in preparing my manuscripts for publication.

Finally, I remind the reader that this book is not a publication of The Church of Jesus Christ of Latter-day Saints nor of Brigham Young University. Though I believe the content to be accurate, I bear sole responsibility for what follows.

Introduction

As a seventeen- or eighteen-year-old boy, I remember asking myself the question, "If I died today, would I go to heaven or hell?" I suppose all of us have asked ourselves this same thing; and in all probability, on more than one occasion. Sadly, I fear, too many really aren't sure what the answer would be. Robert L. Millet has conjectured that if you asked ten people, "If you were to die this minute . . . where would you go? at least seven out of ten persons would sheepishly respond: 'I don't know. I suppose the terrestrial kingdom?'"[1] Such should not be the case—particularly among those who have abiding testimonies of the restored gospel of Jesus Christ. One might argue that perhaps we're not *supposed* to be sure—at least not until we make our calling and election sure. However, that seems unlikely. The Lord, through His Spirit, is constantly giving us reassurances of His satisfaction with our progress. And His nature—as the ultimate Father—is to encourage His children, particularly when they are progressing and doing as He wishes. True, we are to work out "[our] salvation with fear and trembling" (Philippians 2:12), but it is my firm belief that the Lord wants us to know if we're on the right path. I believe He wants us to know that, if we are pressing forward, we *will* gain exaltation. None of us, *ever,* are doing *all* we can or should. But the Lord's atonement will compensate for our deficiencies, if we are sincerely trying to daily improve our lives and our natures. Of course, a person who stops trying because he or she thinks that salvation is assured would not, in the end, be exalted. And, similarly, a person filled with fear and doubt as to whether exaltation is attainable is likely to get discouraged and also give up trying. Thus, assurances from the Lord regarding His pleasure at our progress tend to be accompanied by subtle spiritual promptings regarding areas in which we can do better. But my contention is that the Lord does not wish us to be "in the dark," per se, about our spiritual productivity and growth.

Some years ago, while renewing my temple recommend (with a member of my stake presidency), I was asked the last of the recommend questions, which at that time read: "Do you consider yourself worthy in every way to enter the temple . . . ?" I responded, with enthusiasm, "Absolutely!"—to which the good brother interviewing me appeared genuinely shocked. I felt as though I had actually made him uncomfortable, perhaps more so than if I had confessed some serious transgression. When I queried as to why he looked so puzzled, he said that very few of the individuals he had interviewed over the years had responded in the affirmative, without some hesitancy or clarification, such as, "Well,

I'm trying" or "I do my best." My optimistic response, he said, simply caught him off guard. So I asked, "President, am I wrong to feel that way? Should I be less certain about my worthiness or acceptability before the Lord?" He assured me that was not the case, and that he was just not used to members of the stake feeling so confident that they were living as the Lord desired. That experience has stuck with me and has caused me time and again to ask myself why this would be the case—why are so few members of the Church uncertain about how well they are doing in the quest for eternal life?

This book was born out of a manifest recurring concern that too many do not feel confident that they are going to "make it" to the celestial kingdom.

Will I be exalted?
Can I do all that is required of me?
Can I become perfect?
Have I fully repented of every sin?
How can I ever be as good as the prophets and apostles?
How can I know if I'm on the right path?

Questions such as these are common among members of the Church. A seemingly large percentage of us tend to wonder whether we're really capable of doing all that is necessary to merit a place in that highest of heavenly rewards. In my view, that pessimism or uncertainty is born less of a sense of unworthiness and more of a misunderstanding of God's great plan and what it is the Lord actually expects of us. Nonetheless, I can't imagine traversing

70 plus years of mortality—with all of its accompanying trials and tests—with such a nebulous and doubt-filled perspective with regard to my acceptability before God, let alone with regard to His love (or lack thereof) for me. As Robert L. Millet once noted: "Though we dare not face life with pride or immoderate self-assurance, we must also avoid false modesty and doubt, which are antithetical to faith. Joseph Smith taught that doubt—including a constant worry about our standing before God or our capacity to go where Christ is—cannot coexist with saving faith (*Lectures on Faith,* 3:20–21; 4:13; 6:12)."[2] Elder Russell M. Nelson of the Quorum of the Twelve Apostles reminds us: "When comparing one's personal performance with the supreme standard of the Lord's expectation, the reality of imperfection can at times be depressing. My heart goes out to conscientious Saints who, because of their shortcomings, allow feelings of depression to rob them of happiness in life. We all need to remember: men are that they might have joy—not guilt trips!"[3]

What follows is my perception of God's nature, His plan, and our odds of being exalted—based on what ancient and modern prophets and apostles have taught! Perhaps you see things differently. But I invite you to explore with me what the Lord has revealed on this vital topic—as it is my sincere hope that you too will feel of the functionality of the Lord's plan.

As we begin this little theological journey together, I must acknowledge at the onset that every coin has two sides. No matter what the gospel topic, there is always a negative and a positive side—the dos and the don'ts, the consequences for breaking a commandment and the blessings that are promised to those who keep it. So it is with the subject at hand. Our focus here is on God's mercy and grace and the functionality of the Father's plan of salvation. Part of that discussion *could* be an exploration of what will happen to those who do *not* follow God's commands or what the day of judgment will be like for those who lived lives of sin and willful disobedience. Those are germane topics, but they are not our subject here. Rather, my message is a positive one—not one of doom and gloom or hellfire and damnation. President Brigham Young once remarked: "You can put into a gnat's eye all the souls of the children of men that are driven into heaven by preaching hell-fire."[4] I deeply resonate with that optimistic approach to the gospel. Thus, this will not be a book about the consequences of sin. We will not be discussing the rebellious, the sinful, the innately evil, or the unrepentant. This book is about one side of the coin: the side that pertains to those who really do want to keep the commandments—those who are honestly seeking each day to be better, more Christlike, more holy. To those, this book is directed. And on that subject this book has its focus.

I have tried to rely primarily upon the scriptures for my understanding. And I have drawn heavily on words spoken under the direction of the Holy Spirit by those whose words constitute scripture (see D&C 68:4). President Boyd K. Packer once noted: "Individual doctrines of the gospel are not fully explained in one place in the scriptures, nor presented in order or sequence. They must be assembled from pieces here and there. They are sometimes found in large segments, but mostly they are in small bits scattered through the chapters and verses."[5] Such is certainly the case with the doctrines of the plan of salvation—and particularly with the statistical odds that it will exalt both you and me. Thus, I have done my best to "assemble" some of the pieces the General Authorities have offered us on this sacred subject; all in the hopes that this small work will build faith—faith in God's plan, in His Son's atonement, and in the Holy Spirit's power to change and cleanse lives. In the end, it is my desire to instill in the reader a greater sense of the unfailing love, mercy, and work of God on our behalf—and a greater sense of God's power and desire to exalt *all* of His children.

CHAPTER ONE

The Role of Commandments

Since the very beginnings of the restoration of the gospel of Jesus Christ a tension has existed between the role played by works and that of grace in the salvation of God's children.

True, the Mormon faith "grew up," so to speak, in a predominantly Protestant milieu—and its worship forms clearly mirror that. Nonetheless, views of salvation among Latter-day Saints tend to parallel early twentieth-century Catholic approaches or those of puritanical Protestant beliefs rather than those found in the evangelical Christian movement. Thus, many Latter-day Saints are much more likely to talk about their need to be obedient to covenants and commandments than they are to speak of the exalting grace of God and His Christ.

This tension between grace and works is not altogether a bad thing. Indeed, a congregation that emphasizes good works as the primary means of salvation will likely be made up of overwhelmed and potentially dispirited parishioners. And the opposite is also true; if the emphasis on how one gains salvation is placed entirely upon grace it is likely that complacency and a lack of personal righteousness will be the outcome. Thus, it is imperative that emphasis be placed on *both* grace and works. Neither operating in a vacuum; neither functional on its own; each dependent upon the other. We must recognize that grace and works are not opposites, but rather two ends of the same stick; two facets of the same eternal plan; two necessary parts of the same redemptive act—the atoning sacrifice of the Lord Jesus Christ.

In the restored gospel, grace and works ever go hand in hand. No one will *ever* be exalted by the grace of the Lord Jesus Christ, if that person is complacent in his approach to the commandments. Nor will anyone find himself exalted solely through seeking to keep *all* of the commandments of Christ, as *no one* is able to *fully* do so.[1] Indeed, no one (except Jesus) even comes close to keeping *all* of the commandments. Of course, the principle we are discussing will not be new to the reader. It is a foundational component in accurately understanding the atonement of the Lord Jesus Christ. Nevertheless, the interplay between these two related forces—grace and works—is occasionally neglected in dialogues about salvation. Sadly, sometimes contentious arguments about who God will save, and how He will save them, are the result of such misunderstandings. Consequently, over the two millennia since Jesus established the Christian faith, many who profess the Christian conviction have, nonetheless, been less than Christ-like to their fellow brothers and sisters in the faith because of divergent views on the issue of grace vs. works. Such should not be the case.

Many centuries before the Protestant Reformation and the subsequent restoration of the gospel, the Christian church was quite clear on the relationship between grace and works. Church fathers from both the Latin and Greek traditions explained the interconnectedness of these two components of salvation in words very similar to the Book of Mormon proclamation: "It is by grace that we are saved, after all we can do" (2 Nephi 25:23). In his book, *Early Christian Doctrines,* patristic scholar J. N. D. Kelly offered the following explanation as to how early Christians perceived the roles of grace and works:

> Our salvation comes, stated Gregory Nazianzen, both from ourselves and from God. If God's help is necessary for doing good and if the good will itself comes from Him, it is equally true that the initiative rests with man's free will. [John] Chrysostom similarly teaches that without God's aid we should be unable to accomplish good works; nevertheless, even if grace takes the lead, it co-operates with free will. We first of all begin to desire the good and to incline ourselves towards it, and then God steps in to strengthen that desire and render it effective . . . So Ambrose states, "In everything the Lord's power cooperates with man's efforts"; but he can also say, "Our free will gives us either a propensity to virtue or an inclination to sin." In numerous passages he lays it down that the grace of salvation will only come to those who make the effort to bestir themselves . . . Theodoret's

> view is that, while all men need grace and it is impossible to take a step on the road to virtue without it, the human will must collaborate with it. "There is need," he writes, "of both our efforts and the divine succour. The grace of the Spirit is not vouchsafed to those who make no effort, and without that grace our efforts cannot collect the prize of virtue."[2]

Thus we see that the early Christians commonly held that one was exalted *entirely* by grace, but that works vouchsafed that grace, enabling the practitioner to lay hold upon it, or qualify for it. Grace could not be earned, according to early Christians. But it wasn't given to those who made no effort either.

Similarly, the LDS position is that our works cannot save us but are necessary (1) as a manifestation of true or sincere faith, and (2) in order that we might become like God, as we have been commanded to be (see Matthew 5:48). Only the works of Jesus Christ can actually save or exalt.[3] Men's personal works have no power to redeem them—as we can never do sufficient good to override both our sins and also our all-encompassing dependence upon God and Christ. Additionally, it is a fallacy to say that Jesus saves us, but then our works exalt us—an idea I have heard expressed not a few times by members of the Church. That too implies a self-sufficiency that is, at best, damning! Thus, King Benjamin reminds us:

> And now, in the first place, he hath created you, and granted unto you your lives, for which ye are indebted unto him. And secondly, he doth require that ye should do as he hath commanded you; for which if ye do, he doth

> immediately bless you; and therefore he hath paid you. And ye are still indebted unto him, and are, and will be, forever and ever; therefore, of what have ye to boast? (Mosiah 2:23–24)

King Benjamin informs us that we are ever indebted to God and Christ for (1) forgiving us of our sins, and also (2) for blessing us for our meager efforts to be obedient. And, he points out, we are eternally beholden to Him for our very lives. King Benjamin had previously said:

> I say unto you, my brethren, that if you should render all the thanks and praise which your whole soul has power to possess, to that God who has created you, and has kept and preserved you, and has caused that ye should rejoice, and has granted that ye should live in peace one with another—I say unto you that if ye should serve him who has created you from the beginning, and is preserving you from day to day, by lending you breath, that ye may live and move and do according to your own will, and even supporting you from one moment to another—I say, if ye should serve him with all your whole souls yet ye would be *unprofitable servants.* (Mosiah 2:20–21; emphasis added)

What an acknowledgment! We are unprofitable servants! Although we acknowledge the Lord's declaration regarding the great worth of souls in the eyes of God (see D&C 18:10), nevertheless, here King Benjamin highlights our cost rather than our worth! And what do we cost? According to scripture, more than we're worth! We are, each of us, a drain on the system! In the fullest sense, we are not contributors but, rather, more like leeches! Although the message hardly sounds uplifting, on the contrary, uplifting is exactly what it is! With all of the things King Benjamin stated as absolute truth—namely that we are inadequate and continually indebted to God and Christ—yet They still bless us. They still love us. They still guide and protect us. And They have every intent of exalting us, if we desire that it be so. What a profound promise! What an illuminating statement about the nature and depth of divine grace and mercy!

In what appears to be an effort to give context and parameters to God's expressed loved, we are wont to quote 2 Nephi 25:23, which reads: "We know that it is by grace that we are saved, after all we can do." Too often we misinterpret this to mean that we have to do everything possible—everything within our power—and *then* God's grace will kick in. Many see Nephi's words as a caution, rather than a promise—as though Nephi is saying you do the impossible, and then—and only then—go talk to God about offering you a little help.[4] If that is really what Nephi means, then Jesus will be the only saved being, as He is the only one who has done *all* He possibly could. But this is not what the passage is teaching. What Nephi is telling us is that it is still by God's grace that we will be saved—even if we do the very best we can. And why is that the case? Because "all we can do" is inconsequential in comparison to all God does and all that needs to be done. In other words, our meager offering is simply not enough to save or exalt us! Thus, *Christ* is our Savior. Not our small acts of faithfulness. One commentator paraphrased 2 Nephi 25:23 as follows: "We are saved by grace 'apart from all we can do,' or . . . 'regardless of all we can do.' Another acceptable paraphrase of the sense of the verse might read, 'We are still saved by grace, after all is said and done.'"[5] Simply put, we cannot separate grace and works, but in the combination of the two, we *cannot* place the emphasis on *our* works, but rather on *Christ's*. For, even if we expend all of our best efforts, it will take Jesus' love, concern, righteousness, and power to redeem us from our fallen condition. And yet, that was always the plan!

Let us not forget that the commandments we have been given predate mortality. They predate the fall of Adam and Eve. They existed before you and I were born as spirits in heavenly realms to loving Heavenly Parents. Indeed, they are eternal.[6] They are the laws by which all humans who ever have lived, or ever will live, will be judged and potentially exalted.[7] The very laws you and I have been given as commandments are the same laws our Father in Heaven successfully obeyed during His mortal probation. The Prophet Joseph stated:

> *It is the first principle of the Gospel to know for a certainty the Character of God, and to know that we may converse with him as one man converses with another, and that he was once a man like us; yea, that God himself, the Father of us all, dwelt on an earth, the same as Jesus Christ himself did* . . . and you have got to learn how to be Gods yourselves, and to be kings

and priests to God, the same as all Gods have done before you.[8]

Similarly, Elder James E. Talmage of the Council of the Twelve Apostles stated: "The Eternal Father . . . was once a Man, and has progressed, not by any favor but *by* the right of *conquest over sin,* and over death, to His present position of priesthood and power, of Godship and Godliness, as the Supreme Being whom we all profess to worship."[9] President Brigham Young taught this same idea on numerous occasions, stating that God the Father "has passed the ordeals we are now passing through; . . . *he has passed through the whole of it,* and has received his crown and exaltation."[10] President George Q. Cannon, a counselor to three different presidents of the Church, taught: "The exaltation which God has attained to has been *through obedience to these self-same laws that are now taught to us.*"[11] And Elder Bruce R. McConkie wrote this: "The Father . . . worked out his salvation *by obedience to the same laws he has given to us* so that we may do the same."[12]

The laws and ordinances by which men and women are exalted in the celestial kingdom of our God are eternal and do not change—and because they are eternal, they predate even God.[13] Yes, they have always existed and have ever been operative. And no, they are not negotiable. All beings are saved on the same principles—by the same laws and ordinances—in all dispensations, on every earth created by the great God who "upholds all worlds and all things by his power."[14] But it is imperative to understand that, although we are all judged by the same laws, our circumstances influence what is expected of us individually under those laws.

From the very beginning of the Plan's institution, we each understood that we would have less ability than Jesus to keep the Father's commandments. That is why we were taught that an important part of the Plan was the Father's intention to provide us a Savior. We trusted in that promise and certainly rejoiced at the announcement. Our inequality with Christ made this a necessary component of the Father's plan. Likewise, you and I are also unequal in our individual abilities to keep the commandments, when compared to each other. Instructively, in Jesus' parable of the talents (see Matthew 25:14–30) the Lord rewards all his servants equally, even though not all were equally productive. Only the entirely unproductive were dismissed as worthless. It becomes clear in the parable that the reward was not based on how much one did, but rather what one did with what he was given. So it is with us. As Elder James E. Talmage put it:

> Both the servant who had been entrusted with five talents and he who had received but two were equally commended, and, as far as we are told, were equally recompensed. The talents bestowed upon each were the gift of his Lord, who knew well whether that servant was capable of using to better advantage one, two, or five. Let no one conclude that good work of relatively small scope is less necessary or acceptable than like service of wider range. Many a man who has succeeded well in business with small capital would have failed in

> the administration of vast sums; so also in spiritual achievements 'there are diversities of gifts, but the same Spirit.'
>
> Of the man endowed with many talents greater returns were expected.[15]

Likewise, D. Kelly Ogden and Andrew C. Skinner have written:

> The parable is not about three levels of goodness but about doing the best we can with what we've been given. (As our leaders have often counseled us, it is not *where* we serve but *how* we serve that matters.) The servant who doubled his two talents earned the same reward as he who doubled the five talents. They were both faithful, and the faithful, in the end, will be given all the Father has.[16]

God expects us to seek to be faithful to Him in the stewardship He has given us and conscientious in how we use the talents and gifts He has endowed us with (see Alma 29:6–7). I am not called to be a faithful president of the Church. I am simply called to be as faithful as I can in my small stewardship in my small portion of the vineyard. If the president of the Church is faithful in his stewardship, and I in mine, we will both receive the same reward; namely eternal life in the presence of God.

Of course, there is the great dilemma that all of us face. No one—no, not one—is capable of living the commandments fully. No one, save Christ only! From the very hour the commandments were explained to us in the premortal world it was known by all present that we would not be capable of living them to the degree that the law of justice demands—to the degree one must in order to be exalted. It is for this very reason that the Father provided as part of His plan a Savior, a Redeemer, a Messiah. From the foundations of the world the Father chose and foreordained His Only Begotten Son to ransom us all (see 1 Peter 1:20), worlds without end (see Moses 1:33–35). In so doing, He insured that the impossible would become a reality. We would be exalted! Mercy could not rob justice. But Jesus had within Himself the nature and power to satisfy the demands of justice, thereby making mercy an available gift to all who desire it.[17]

What then must we know about commandments? We must believe they are always given for our safety, protection, growth, and happiness. And we must—with all our hearts—seek to keep them! But they are not given as the primary means of obtaining our exaltation. If that were the case, again, none would be exalted, with the sole exception of Jesus the Christ. Commandments and trials offer us the experiences necessary to learn the lessons of life and opportunities to develop the attributes of godhood. They help us to see things, and others, as God sees them. They often provoke in us a spirit of love, forgiveness, and understanding. And they certainly keep us safe and happy. These are the reasons the Father gave us commandments. He did not reveal them out of a desire to damn us. Jesus was foreordained to be the Messiah long before any of us were sent to earth because the Father knew that we not only could not keep all of His commandments, but also because we needed the trials life and sin bring in order to develop spirituality. In this view, the frustrations and failings of life are really blessings in disguise. We could never become like God without them.

Elder Neal A. Maxwell wisely noted:

> The Atonement is there for our daily mistakes. It's understandable that we focus on the major crises. But we sometimes allow ourselves to be overcome by relentless routineness. That can cause a "daily dampening of things spiritual." . . . Being tried means being developed. We don't look at impatience in terms of its downsize. When we are impatient we do not honor what is implied in the words "in process of time." We foolishly wish to have some moments over and done with, ignoring the possibilities of service inherent in them. If we want to "fly over" (so to speak) some experiences, it likely means that we will miss the chance to be of service [and parenthetically, we will miss opportunities for personal growth and development—for which mortality was designed]. Impatience puts us at risk. We may feel "put upon" by events and circumstances. This is another mistake we can make in not approaching the Atonement in order to draw upon it. And yet these things which we feel "put upon" with actually constitute the customized curriculum needed for our personal development. Too often we push away the necessary and prescribed courses of 'spiritual calisthenics.' As if we could withdraw from all of life's courses and still remain enrolled in school.[18]

The trials and challenges of life are a blessing—a gift to us from God. A perfectly lived life must be our goal. But a flawed life, marred by the occasional sin or misstep, also has its place in the divine Plan. So much of what we know, so much of life's "aha's," come from lessons taught to us by our mistakes or shortcomings. These little errors are part of the curriculum God designed for the mortal experience.

The message of the Atonement is this: First, God has prepared a way for us to return to Him. And second, God does not require perfection of us in order for us to gain exaltation. Jesus needed to be perfect. You and I only need to accept and apply His perfection—all the while, seeking to be the best we can. As Paul noted, Jesus, "who knew no sin," took upon Himself our sins "that we might be made the righteousness of God in him" (2 Corinthians 5:21). In other words, in Gethsemane and on Golgotha, Jesus willingly became guilty of our sins so that those of us who were willing to love and follow Him might become inheritors of His righteousness.

President Heber J. Grant taught:

> If we examine the plan of life and salvation, if we examine the commandments that are given to us as members of the Church of God, we will find that each and every one of those commandments has been given for the express purpose that we may be benefitted, that we may . . . go back and dwell in the presence of our Heavenly Father . . . These duties and obligations are calculated to . . . make Gods of us, . . . that we can become joint heirs with our Lord and Savior Jesus Christ and dwell with Him in the presence of God the Eternal Father throughout all the countless ages of eternity.[19]

Similarly, Elder Richard L. Evans of the Quorum of the Twelve once remarked:

> Despite all discouragements, and sometimes despair, there is the blessed reassuring certainty that the Lord God who gave us life and made us in His image will, with our willingness, lead us to further light, to fuller life, and happiness. For this cause were all the commandments given—and for this He sent His only begotten Son not to condemn, but to save the world (See John 3:17) . . . What else would any father wish for his children? What else would we wish for our own—but happiness and everlasting life with our loved ones? And for this cause are all the counsels and commandments of God given.[20]

Elder Bruce C. Hafen of the Seventy wrote this: "The commandments of God are designed for our ultimate happiness."[21] Thus, the role of the commandments is not to judge and condemn, but to guide, to teach, to protect, and to enable us to enjoy all that the Father has to give—both in this life and, more particularly, in the life to come. Thanks be to the Father for sending His Only Begotten Son. And thanks be to the Son for loving us enough to come and do the will of the Father. "I stand all amazed at the love Jesus offers me."[22]

CHAPTER TWO

A Plan That Will Maximize Returns

As Latter-day Saints we speak freely and often about the "Plan of Salvation" or, perhaps better put, the "Plan *for* Salvation." Indeed, sacred scripture gives this divine "Plan" many names. Elder Boyd K. Packer compiled the following list of scriptural titles for Heavenly Father's Plan:

> The merciful plan of the great Creator (see 2 Nephi 9:6).
> The plan of mercy (see Alma 42:15).
> The plan of mercy (see Alma 42:31).
> The great plan of redemption (see Jacob 6:8; Alma 12:25–26, 30, 32; 17:16; 18:39; 22:13–14; 29:2; 39:18; 42:11, 13).
> The eternal plan of redemption (see Alma 34:16).
> The great plan of redemption (see Alma 34:31).
> The plan of salvation (see Jarom 1:2; Alma 24:14; 42:5; Moses 6:62).
> The plan of our God (see 2 Nephi 9:13).

The great plan of the Eternal God (see Alma 34:9).
The eternal plan of deliverance (see 2 Nephi 11:5).
The plan of happiness (see Alma 42:16).
The great plan of happiness (see Alma 42:8).
The plan of restoration (see Alma 41:2).
The plan of the Gods (see Abraham 4:21).[1]

These many titles define the nature of the Plan. Among other things, we learn that it is great, merciful, eternal, redemptive, salvific, restorative, and greatly promoting of our happiness. It is not the "awful plan of damnation," the "plan of misery," or the "eternal plan of punishment." It was not designed for the purpose of punishing or damning us—nor was it implemented to bring us misery and suffering. To the contrary, the purpose of the Plan—the whole purpose for which it was created and introduced—was the salvation and exaltation of all mankind![2] God offered it as a gift to you and me—a token of His divine, deep, and abiding love for each of His children and for all of His creations. He sought to give us what He has by creating a plan that could make us like He is. We are the blessed recipients of this most wonderful of all designs.

Typically, when we give a gift to someone we love, we want to give the best we have. If we decide to make or create the gift ourselves, we try our hardest to make it the best our skill will allow. If we purchase it, we want to buy the best our personal finances will allow. In this sense, the Father is no different than you and I. He has created and offered to us a great gift—eternal redemption and exaltation. Because God is perfect, His plan for accomplishing His goal is perfect—and thus we could not hope for a better plan. Because He is loving, the gift is given out of love and is ideal (or perfect, complete, nothing lacking), just as His love is ideal, perfect, complete, nothing lacking.

We must remember—and we *must* firmly believe—that the plan of salvation, the great plan of happiness, was designed to work. Indeed, it would not be called the eternal plan of salvation/happiness/redemption/mercy/deliverance/etc. if it did not work—particularly if its primary effect was the damnation of the vast majority of God's offspring. From an LDS position, to be damned is to be stopped in one's progression (i.e., to be forever in a non-exalted state).[3] It intuitively goes against everything we know about the nature of God to suggest that He would create and institute a plan that would, *by design,* damn *most* of His children. Yes, agency must be preserved. But to design a plan that is so difficult to succeed at that most would fail does not preserve agency. On the contrary, such would thwart both agency and the very thing the Plan was created to accomplish—namely, our exaltation. The thought that God would promote something that would ensure that the vast majority of His children would never again be able to dwell in His presence is incomprehensible. And the assumption that our mother in heaven would idly sit back and allow such a guaranteed flop to eternally strip her of any interaction with her spirit offspring is equally unfathomable. Such could not—and did not—happen!

Additionally, we know that upon having the Plan introduced

to us in the premortal world, we were so happy at what the Father was telling us, you and I shouted for joy. We often quote the book of Job, which reads: "The morning stars sang together, and all the sons of God shouted for joy" (Job 38:7). Of this verse, President J. Reuben Clark Jr. wrote that it "could well have been the acclaim that came in the Grand Council when the decision was reached to create an earth where those assembled might come . . . that they might ' . . . have glory added upon their heads for ever and ever.' (Abraham 3:26.)"[4] Elder B. H. Roberts wrote: "It is not unlikely that the shouting of all the sons of God for joy, at the creation of the earth was in consequence of the prospects which opened before these spirits because of the earth-life and the salvation that would come to them through the gospel—even in the prospects of that 'eternal life, which God, that cannot lie, promised before the world began.'"[5] Clearly, those of us who shouted for joy sensed that what God was telling us was good and desirable. Clearly, we felt that the odds were in our favor. There is no sense of foreboding or fear present in the language of scripture. We shouted for joy—not out of fear! If the Father had informed us that "there's good news and bad news"—and had He continued, "The good news is there is a Plan, but the bad news is *most* of you are not going to make it back . . ."—surely we would not have felt reason to rejoice. But that is not what happened. The Father literally introduced us to good news: the good news that He had a plan that would readily make us like Him, and the good news that Christ would be sent to atone for our weaknesses and failings. We saw this as a win/win situation.[6] We knew we wouldn't be perfect, but we knew that the Father's Plan would provide a remedy.

All too often we assume that only a small, select few will return to the Father's presence, there to dwell with Him for time and for all eternity. Yes, only the select will have the honor and privilege of so doing. But who is it that the Father has selected for this great blessing? Our answer—*all* of His children! The Father desires that *all* be exalted. Not just saved, but exalted! He desires that *all* return to Him to dwell with Him for eternity. He made it clear in the Grand Council before the world was that the Plan has the power and potential to exalt *all* of us—not just a few lucky ones, or a small number of the exceedingly faithful. Indeed, modern prophetic declarations make it quite clear that more of God's children will be exalted than will be lost.[7]

In 1976, one of the most doctrinally conservative voices to bear the prophetic mantle in this dispensation,[8] Elder Bruce R. McConkie, said the following to a group of Church Educational System employees gathered in Salt Lake City: "You tell your students that far more of our Father's children will be exalted than we think!"[9] Many present were surprised, as was evidenced by the audible eruption that immediately rippled through the room. The response was not a negative one—just one of surprise. Most were elated. And yet most had traditionally not thought in such optimistic terms, even though by profession it was their job to spread the "good news" of Christ's saving ministry. Elder McConkie was asked by one then present to explain what exactly he meant by this comment, to which he replied:

> All faithful Latter-day Saints—those who chart their course toward eternal life, receive the ordinances of salvation, and strive with all their hearts to be true to their covenants—will gain eternal life. Even though they are certainly not perfect when they die, if they have sought to stay on course, in covenant, in harmony with the mind and will of God, they will be saved in the highest heaven. . . . We ought to have hope, [and] we [need] to be positive and optimistic about attaining that glory.[10]

Indeed, time and again, Elder McConkie made similar comments about his optimistic view of God's Plan for our exaltation. He said: "If we chart a course of becoming perfect, and, step by step and phase by phase, are perfecting our souls by overcoming the world, then it is absolutely guaranteed—there is no question whatever about it—we shall gain eternal life."[11] He also taught:

> If we chart a course and follow it to the best of our ability in this life, then when we go out of this life we'll continue in exactly that same course. We will no longer be subject to the passions and the appetites of the flesh. We will have passed successfully the tests of this mortal probation and in due course we'll get the fulness of our Father's kingdom—and that means eternal life in his everlasting presence.[12]

Addressing a large audience of practicing Latter-day Saints, Elder McConkie once said: "I would suppose . . . that I am now looking out upon a group of men and women who will all go to the celestial kingdom."[13] He also rhetorically asked, "Who can count the number of saved beings in eternity? Our God, who is triumphant in all battles against the forces of evil, will surely be victorious in the numbers of his children who will be saved."[14] Time and again Elder McConkie declared: "Good and faithful members of the Church will be saved [by which I mean exalted] even though they are far from perfect in this life."[15]

It should be noted that Elder McConkie is not the only Latter-day Saint with a witness of this optimistic view of the Father's Plan and its power to save us. Robert L. Millet, former dean of Religious Education at Brigham Young University, wrote: "There is no ceiling on the number of saved beings in eternity, no cap, no quota by which the Father of us all must and will be governed. Like any parent, he surely desires that all of his sons and daughters receive the message of salvation, work righteousness, and return to him honorably. Not all will, it is true. But many will—a great many."[16] Along with Brother Millet, Brent L. Top (former associate dean of Religious Education at BYU), and Joseph Fielding McConkie (professor of ancient scripture at BYU) penned this: "Let us reason for a moment. In comparison to the number of wicked souls *at any given time,* perhaps the numbers of faithful followers seem small. But we must keep in mind how many of our spirit brothers and sisters—almost an infinite number—will be saved."[17] Brother Joseph McConkie once wrote: "Of those who kept their first estate and gained the privilege of being born into mortality the vast majority will return to the presence of their heavenly parents to receive the fulness of their divine inheritance."[18] Indeed, simple logic would suggest: "Our God and Father is a successful parent, one who will save far more of his children than he will lose!"[19] Stephen E. Robinson and H. Dean Garrett wrote: "Those who inherit the celestial kingdom will find themselves in communion and fellowship with billions upon billions of celestial beings like themselves—the hosts of heaven—from billions upon billions of other worlds all created and glorified by the same Jesus Christ who created our world and who will glorify us."[20]

In the book *Revelations of the Restoration* we find the following insight:

> It is a false notion, one not worthy of the gospel of Jesus Christ, that only a few of God's children will be saved in the kingdom of God. In his vision of the redemption of the dead, President Joseph F. Smith saw an "innumerable company of the spirits of the just, who had been faithful in the testimony of Jesus while they lived in mortality" (D&C 138:12). All these awaited a glorious resurrection—and their number was limited to those who had lived from the days of Adam to the time of the crucifixion of Christ. Similarly, Alma spoke of "many, exceedingly great many, who were made pure and entered into the rest of the Lord their God" (Alma 13:12). Paul told the faithful of his day that they would join "an innumerable company of angels" in the heavenly place (Hebrews 12:22), while Daniel numbered the righteous who would stand before God as a "thousand thousands" who ministered to him, "and ten thousand times ten thousand"

> who stood before him (Daniel 7:10). When Christ said, "In my Father's house [kingdom] are many mansions: if it were not so, I would have told you. I go to prepare a place for you" (John 14:2; see also Smith, *History of the Church,* 4:184), he was not suggesting that there were various degrees of glory. At that moment he was speaking to the Twelve, and though one of them would betray him, he was giving them the assurance that there was room for them and as many as would believe on their word in his Father's kingdom. There is no boundary to the heavenly city, no limit that needs to be put on its population. There is room in his Father's kingdom for every one of his children, if they will but choose to abide there. Were this not the case, were it true that God did not desire to save all of his children, Christ said, "I would have told you" (John 14:2).[21]

In Revelation 19:1 we read: "And after these things I heard a great voice of much people in heaven, saying, Alleluia; Salvation, and glory, and honour, and power, unto the Lord our God" (see also Revelation 5:11; 7:9). Note that John says that there were many, or "much people in heaven." Clearly, we should not assume that most of God's children are going to be damned.[22] Indeed, those of us who truly believe in Christ and have faith in His atoning sacrifice *must* believe that many, many of God's children will be exalted in the celestial kingdom![23]

Of course we do not dismiss scriptural declarations that clearly and accurately describe our personal pathetic circumstances. For example, the apostle Paul informed us: "They are all gone out of the way, they are together become unprofitable; there is none that doeth good, no, not one" (Romans 3:12). Similarly, in Mosiah 2:21 we read: "I say unto you that if ye should serve him who has created you from the beginning, and is preserving you from day to day, by lending you breath, that ye may live and move and do according to your own will, and even supporting you from one moment to another—I say, if ye should serve him with all your whole souls yet ye would be unprofitable servants." Truly, as human beings saturated in weakness (see Ether 12:27) simply by virtue of the mortal experience, we are inconsequential in and of ourselves. But the Plan does not leave us to ourselves. We are partnered with Christ. And that alone gives us infinite worth. Thus, although we may be imperfect, unimpressive, or incapable of saving ourselves, God and Christ are not incapable of doing for us what we cannot do ourselves. And we have their love, power, and promises to both guide and preserve us.

But how is it to be done? How will God and Christ exalt more than they will lose in a world seemingly filled with wickedness and sin? Is such a grand promise of so many saved creations from a fallen world realistic, particularly when scripture informs us that God "cannot look upon sin with the least degree of allowance"? (Alma 45:16; D&C 1:31).

Oh, the greatness of the Plan! Oh, the wisdom of our God! Oh, the forethought He and His Son had in the grand councils before the world was! All has been considered. And all arrangements have been made. We left the presence of the Father, to begin our mortal journey, with the absolute assurance and with complete confidence that the Plan the Father was inviting us to participate in was safe, good, helpful, and exalting. And so it is!

A number of revealed truths lead us to a belief that the Plan works and that you and I likely will be exalted:

- the merciful, loving, and benevolent nature of the Father
- the perfect Atonement wrought by the Son
- the nature and length of the mortal experience
- high infant mortality rates, coupled with the truth that children are not accountable for sin
- Satan is to be bound during the Millennium

All these things, and many more, assure us that the Plan is perfect, that everything has been taken into consideration, and that you and I will likely be exalted.

Infant Mortality Rates

Thankfully, today, in westernized nations that enjoy ongoing medical advancements, most children survive both childbirth and infancy. Indeed, statistically speaking, most children born in the twenty-first century will live beyond the age of eight—the age of accountability. But such has not always been the case. One need only look back 100 years to see a dramatic increase in infant mortality in comparison to today's trends.

Consider this. In the United States in 1910, one out of every ten babies died before its first birthday. Even as recently as 1970 the worldwide average for children dying prior to their fifth birthday was approximately 15 percent—that's 15 percent of all children born upon this planet. Although, as of 2004, the rate of premature deaths worldwide had dropped to around 8 percent; nonetheless, in countries such as Sierra Leone, Niger, or Angola, the statistics are still saddening. For example, Sierra Leone had a 36 percent infant mortality rate in 1970. In 2004 the rate of children dying before their fifth birthday in that nation was still at a staggering 28 percent.[24] One study looking at mortality rates of European children within their first year of life suggests that between the early 1500s and the year 1820, approximately 25 percent of all European children lived less than one year.[25] This same study indicates that by age five almost 40 percent of European children died during that same era.[26] In Roman Egypt (A.D. 12–259) more than 33 percent of all children died before the end of their first year of life.[27] It is assumed that these numbers are actually low, because, as one scholar of demography noted, "There was a widespread tendency . . . not to register the burial of an unbaptized infant."[28] A 1973 study concluded that 30–50 percent of all prehistoric and modern, nonindustrialized peoples died prior to adulthood. Indeed, those dying prior to their fifteenth birthday are estimated to be 58.1 percent of the population.[29] What of the underdeveloped or third-world countries? Surely their infant mortality rates were much higher. Indeed, President John Taylor stated that, statistically speaking, the total number of people who have died prior to the age of accountability is "more than one-half of the human family."[30] More than 50 percent!

One scholar has observed:

> Although the chances of death were overall higher for everyone in the past, the main reason life expectancy was so much lower than today was severe infant mortality. In many historical populations between a fourth [25%] and a third [33%] of newborn infants died in their first year of life . . . Estimating the life expectancy of specific historical populations is difficult, but enough evidence has accrued to permit life expectancies to be estimated for a wide range of human populations from prehistoric, to ancient, to modern times. . . . Using model life tables we find that in a population with a female life expectancy of twenty-five years about thirty percent of newborn infants will die in their first year of life. And in this population a female at age fifteen has a fifty percent chance of living to see her fiftieth birthday. . . . In a population with a female life expectancy of twenty-five years, women surviving to age fifty needed to have had about 5.1 live births on average in order to keep the population at level numbers.[31]

What has happened to the more than 50 percent of all of God's children who have died prior to the age of accountability? The holy scriptures and the teachings of the living prophets on this question are quite clear. In a revelation given in 1836, the Lord gave Joseph Smith a glimpse into the celestial kingdom and declared: "All children who die before they arrive at the years of accountability are saved in the celestial kingdom of heaven" (D&C 137:10). And in an epistle written by Mormon to his son Moroni we read: "I [the Lord] am filled with charity, which is everlasting love; wherefore, all children are alike unto me; wherefore, I love little children with a perfect love; and they are all alike and partakers of salvation" (Moroni 8:17; see vv. 5–22). President Joseph Fielding Smith taught: "It does not make any difference whether it is a Catholic baby, a Protestant baby, or a [Muslim] baby: no matter whose baby it is, it is not responsible for original sin; it is not responsible for any sin; and the mercy of God claims it; and it is redeemed."[32] According to President Smith, every child that dies prior to the age of eight will receive a reward of exaltation in the celestial kingdom of God.[33] LDS commentators Hyrum M. Smith (of the Council of the Twelve) and Janne M. Sjodahl wrote: "The celestials must also be numerous, since [all] departed infants belong to that class."[34] Likewise, Elder Bruce R. McConkie wrote:

> Millions of children, from Adamic times to our day, have died before they arrived at the age of accountability, and, because they were alive in Christ and had never died spiritually, they shall have eternal life. It will come to them through the Atonement of Christ. They never were called upon to undergo and overcome the trials and temptations that almost overpower us. Billions of spirits will come to earth during the Millennium, when Satan is bound, when there is peace on earth, when there is no sorrow because there is no death, when they will not be confronted with the evil and carnality

> that face us. They will grow up without sin unto salvation. Thus saith the holy word.[35]

A number of years ago I sat in a high priests group meeting in a ward of which I was not a member. The discussion that particular Sunday was from the Joseph F. Smith *Teachings of Presidents of the Church* manual. The instructor read the following statement from the manual:

> Little children who are taken away in infancy and innocence before they have reached the years of accountability . . . are redeemed, and Satan has no power over them. Neither has death any power over them. They are redeemed by the blood of Christ, and they are saved . . . Such children are in the bosom of the Father. They will inherit their glory and their exaltation, and they will not be deprived of the blessings that belong to them . . . They will lose nothing by being taken away from us in this way.[36]

After reading this quotation the instructor indicated that President Smith's point was that *all* children who die before the age of eight will be exalted.

At this point one of the brethren in the class raised his hand and objected, stating that this seemed unfair and unbelievable. He cited the overwhelming number of children who have died before the age of accountability and then added, "I cannot believe that God could possibly save that many of His children. And I don't see how such could be fair, in light of the fact that they've all died, and you and I are required to remain past the age of eight." Another brother chimed in and expressed a similar sentiment about how unfair this seemed. I was shocked, although not speechless. I raised my hand and expressed my disappointment in the comments of these two brethren. I said, "This should be cause for rejoicing, not jealousy! What a blessing to know that so many are going to be exalted. Yes, you and I have remained. But President Smith's words fill me with hope, not with frustration and anger. Just because we don't understand why we remain when others are taken does not make God's Plan unfair. It only highlights how limited we are in our views."

Elder Bruce R. McConkie reminds us: "Whatever the Lord does is right whether we understand his purposes or not. . . . There will be billions of millennial mortals who will never be tested, as fully as we are, and who will go on to eternal life, as do little children, because an Almighty God in his infinite wisdom arranges that kind of a life for them."[37]

As noted, then, it appears that more than half of all people who have ever lived have died before the age of accountability. And doctrinally speaking, these folks are guaranteed exaltation in the celestial kingdom of God. Yes, they will need to have saving ordinances performed vicariously on their behalf, but they will be saved. There is no doubt about it! And what a testament such news is to God's love and mercy and to the functionality of the Plan He authored!

Now some may ask, "How do we know each of these were supposed to die at an early age? Could any of these deaths have been an accident? Could any of those who died before the age of eight been destined by God to live past the age of accountability, but because of agency, they did not?" To this we answer no! God is in charge and His plans are *never* frustrated. Elder Neal A. Maxwell noted that "no righteous individual dies an untimely death"[38]—and certainly "unaccountable" implies "righteous" in God's eyes. In a modern revelation we read: "Thy days are known, and thy years shall not be numbered less" (D&C 122:9). Elsewhere in the Doctrine and Covenants we are told: "For there is a time appointed for every man, according as his works shall be" (D&C 121:25). Likewise, President Joseph Fielding Smith stated: "No righteous man [or woman] is taken before his [or her] time."[39] From President Spencer W. Kimball we read: "I am positive in my mind that the Lord has planned our destiny. We can shorten our lives [by living recklessly], but I think we cannot lengthen them very much."[40] Elsewhere President Kimball wrote: "Just as Ecclesiastes (3:2) says, I am confident there is a time to die, but I believe also that many people die before 'their time' because they are careless, abuse their bodies, take unnecessary chance, or expose themselves to hazards . . . I believe we may die prematurely [through unrighteous living], but seldom exceed our time very much . . . God controls our lives . . . but gives us our agency. We may . . . foolishly shorten or terminate them." But, if we are living righteously, when our time comes the Lord will take us.[41] President Ezra Taft Benson stated: "It has been said that the death of a righteous person is never untimely because our Father sets the times. I believe that with all my soul."[42]

Those who passed away before the age of accountability did so because such was the plan of God. Obviously, in His eyes they are deemed righteous. Thus their death was not premature. And all of them have been exalted and will dwell for eternity with that same God in His heavens.[43] As Elder Neal A. Maxwell once noted, when we understand that God intends to exalt all who die before the age of accountability, "Infant mortality, which rages in so many parts of the world, is . . . placed in a reassuring doctrinal context (see D&C 137:10)."[44]

The Mentally Handicapped

The good news does not end with the salvation and exaltation of little children who die before the age of eight. The restored gospel also provides a comforting message regarding all those who are born with mental handicaps. President Joseph Fielding Smith put it this way: "Mentally deficient persons, those who are incompetent of understanding, are classed among those who are redeemed as little children through the Atonement of our Redeemer."[45] In the *Encyclopedia of Mormonism* we read: "Latter-day Saints believe in the 'infinite and eternal' power of the Atonement, that it will bring to all mankind an end to the basic effects of the Fall of Adam: it automatically forgives the sins of those who are . . . children under the age of eight, [or] mentally handicapped."[46] It seems reasonable to me that if one who has a mental handicap is on an intellectual level of someone less than eight years of age, that person, upon death, will also be exalted in the celestial kingdom—guaranteed!

Now, although we have no way of calculating how many of God's children have been sent to earth to traverse this mortal experience in a mentally handicapped body, nonetheless, we do know that each has the promise of eternal life. And, more particularly, we realize that this beautiful truth only adds to the numbers of exalted individuals previously cited. Thus, again, an incredibly large number of Father's children will be exalted in the celestial kingdom.

The Millennium

The Millennium will play a significant role in the statistics of which we have been speaking. Why? Because so many will be born during that thousand year period when Satan is bound and righteousness reigns. From *A New Witness for the Articles of Faith* we read: "More people will live on earth during the Millennium than in all prior ages combined many times over."[47] Elsewhere we read:

> What of the countless billions of those children to be born during the great millennial era—during a time when disease and death have no sting nor victory over mankind? This is that time . . . when "children shall grow up without sin unto salvation" (D&C 45:58). Given the renewed and paradisiacal state of the earth, it may well be that more persons will live on the earth during the thousand years of our Lord's reign—persons who are of at least a terrestrial nature—than the combined total of all who have lived

> during the previous six thousand years of the earth's temporal continuance. Indeed, who can count the number of saved beings in eternity? Our God, who is triumphant in all battles against the forces of evil, will surely be victorious in the numbers of his children who will be saved.[48]

In his book *The Millennial Messiah,* Elder McConkie wrote:

> Truly the millennial era is the age of salvation. It has been established by the Lord to save souls. Truly he shall send to earth during that blessed period those who earned the right, by faith and devotion in the premortal life, to receive their mortal probation in a day of peace and righteousness. It is not unreasonable to suppose that more people will live on earth during the millennial era than in all the six millenniums that preceded it combined. And all those who live on the new earth with its new heavens shall be saved. The Lord be praised for his goodness and grace.[49]

In the book of Revelation, John describes the vision he had of the throne of God and the exalted beings who surrounded it. He informs us: "I heard the voice of many angels round about the throne and . . . the number of them was ten thousand times ten thousand, and thousands of thousands" (Revelation 5:11; see also 7:9; 19:1). Of this verse Elder McConkie wrote:

> Lord, are there few that be saved or many (Luke 13:23), is the query in the hearts of many disciples. The answer: Few as compared to the hosts of men in our present worldly

> society (Matt. 7:13–14), but many when all who so obtain are counted together. Here John sees 100,000,000, plus thousands of thousands. Later he shall see "a great multitude [of saved persons], which no man could number." (Rev. 7:9.) The expansion of world population being what it is, we can suppose that the billions who live on earth during the Millennium—and who "grow up without sin unto salvation" (D&C 45:58)—shall far exceed in number the total hosts of men who have lived during the preceding six thousand years. Truly, in the aggregate, there are many who shall be saved![50]

Thus, it appears that during the Millennium—when Satan is bound and we are enabled to live "without sin unto salvation" (D&C 45:58)—righteousness will abound and many, if not most, who live upon the earth during that period of peace will be exalted. If one couples this reality with the unfathomable number of people to be born during the Millennium, the message is one to rejoice over. Again, God has provided the circumstances that will enable a vast number of His children to successfully make their return to His presence. Billions who live during that thousand year period will be exalted. Praise be to the Father and the Son! The Plan works!

Translated Beings

We must not forget to add the inhabitants of the cities of Enoch and Melchizedek to our total of successfully saved beings. During the eras of both of these stalwart and saintly brethren, translation was the norm within the Church.[51] Indeed, likely most from Enoch's Zion, Melchizedek's Salem, and those living in "the golden era of the Nephites," were translated and thus exalted. And how many other "holy societies" have experienced similar things and yet a knowledge of their miracles are lost to us?[52] We have no idea exactly how many of the Saints were sent by the Father to dwell upon the earth during that period of the Church's history. All we can say with certainty is that those who were translated—a number that can conservatively be placed in the millions, if not higher—were all guaranteed exaltation.

The Spirit World

It has become somewhat colloquial to say, "It is ten times harder to accept the gospel in the spirit world than it is to accept it here on earth." It is unclear where this popular saying has its origins.[53] In actuality, there is evidence that the statement is simply untrue.

First of all, since we know that more people will hear the restored gospel in the spirit world than will hear it here on earth—and most of God's children will receive their ordinances vicariously in temples while their spirits dwell in the world of the departed—it makes no sense that acceptance of the gospel in the spirit world will somehow arbitrarily be "ten times harder." For what reason would God make such the case? Particularly since that's the realm where most of His children will be introduced to the truths of Christ's atonement and the restoration of His gospel.[54]

It seems contrary to the nature of God to intentionally put stumbling blocks in front of His children so that they will have difficulty accepting the very thing He sent them to earth to find and embrace.

More to the point, latter-day prophets and apostles have suggested that the gospel is actually readily accepted by those who hear it in the spirit world.[55] For example, in the April 1894 general conference of the Church, President Wilford Woodruff stated: "There will be very few, if any, [in the spirit world] who will not accept the gospel."[56] Likewise, Church patriarch Eldred G. Smith taught that there are constantly "many" in the spirit world who are accepting the gospel; and this has been the case since Christ first introduced it upon His post-mortal visit there.[57] Anthon H. Lund, of the First Presidency, taught that we need to work "in faith" for those in the spirit world. We need to believe that they "will accept the Gospel." "They are longing for the work to be done" on their behalf. Then he added this: "There are many more going to join the ranks of the Saints" in the spirit world, adding dramatically to the numbers of those who accepted the gospel here in morality.[58] President Joseph Fielding Smith taught that, since we who have the gospel are of the house of Israel, then our ancestors who have passed on before us—even if they did not have the gospel—are also of the house of Israel. Thus, according to President Smith, they are "likely to receive the gospel" in the spirit world.[59] John Henry Smith, of the First Presidency, stated that God's "great plan, as revealed to us, provides for the redemption of millions who have gone before without a knowledge of His

Gospel."[60] President Lorenzo Snow taught: "When the Gospel is preached to the spirits in prison, the success attending that preaching will be far greater than that attending the preaching of our Elders in this life. I believe there will be very few indeed of those spirits who will not gladly receive the Gospel when it is carried to them. The circumstances there will be a thousand times more favorable."[61]

In support of all that the Brethren have taught on this subject, there is the confirming witness of personal spiritual experiences. Consider this singular account, which highlights how readily the teaching of the gospel goes forward in the spirit world and how generally vicarious ordinances are accepted by those on whose behalf we perform them. Patriarch Charles Woodbury recorded this experience:

> As I witnessed baptisms one day in the Manti Temple, when the first name was called out for baptism, a voice said to me, "This person has had the gospel taught to him, has accepted it, and desires baptism."
>
> As the second name was read, the voice said: "This person has not heard the gospel yet."
>
> Another name was called, and I was told, "This person has heard the gospel and was not converted."
>
> I witnessed 300 baptisms, each time being advised by the voice as to those who accepted of their baptism, and those who did not. Twenty-five of the 300 whose baptism had been done for them were not ready for it; they had as yet

not been converted to the gospel. The remaining 275 were prepared, and rejoiced that their work was being done.[62]

Many a gospel scholar has conjectured that the conversion process on the other side of the veil is moving forward just as quickly, if not more so, than it is on this side of the sacred divide.[63] If President Woodruff was correct when he said that "very few, if any" in the spirit world would reject the gospel,[64] then Father has indeed done a mighty saving work on behalf of His sons and daughters.[65]

Conclusion

To this point much has been said about the billions upon billions of God's children whom He intends to exalt; and the message thus far has been one of optimism. Nonetheless, you may be asking yourself right about now: "That's great news for all of those groups mentioned. But *I'm* not mentally handicapped, *I* didn't die before the age of accountability, *I'm* not a translated being, *I'm* not living during the Millennium, and *I'm* not being presented the gospel in the spirit world. So what about *me?* What about *my* salvation? Do things merely 'look good' for every group *except for me?* And how, specifically, does all of this optimism translate into *my* personal exaltation?"

These are valid questions. And as we continue our discussion in the chapters that follow, many of these queries will be addressed. Certainly you and I should not assume that we are at a disadvantage because we lived to adulthood, nor should we conjecture that somehow we are unfortunate because we were given the fulness of the gospel of Jesus Christ. Nothing could be further from the truth. As we will note in the chapters that follow, having the gospel places us in an enviable position.

Additionally, it should be pointed out that the very fact that Father's Plan is designed to save so many of these groups mentioned does indirectly say something about your exaltation and mine. After all, we know that the Father is an entirely just and fair God (see Isaiah 45:21; see also Mosiah 2:28; Alma 42:15; 57:26). We know that He is no respecter of persons (see Acts 10:34; see also Moroni 8:12; D&C 1:35; 38:16). Thus, we know God could not create such an optimistic and successful plan for everyone *except* you and me. Because we know that the odds are in favor of exaltation for all those categories we have thus far discussed, we know by default—because of God's nature—that such must also be the case for us. We must believe that for us also, the odds are in our favor! For you and me, things look very good, too! Yes, there are things we must do—and we'll speak of those in the chapters to come. But the hard things have been taken care of by the Father and the Son. What we're called to do is quite easy, in comparison.

Doctrinally speaking, it certainly appears that the Plan was designed to work, that it was created to exalt more individuals than it would damn. Such a doctrine "tastes good" to those who have felt of God's love and "tender mercies" (Psalm 51:1). Such a doctrine brings comfort, reassurance, and a confidence to endure trials. Such a doctrine builds hope and faith. And such a doctrine enables us to see God for what He really is—the ultimate, loving Father.

CHAPTER THREE

THE DOCTRINE OF SANCTIFICATION

As noted in chapter two, literally billions of our Father in Heaven's children have already been guaranteed exaltation in the celestial kingdom. Those who die before the age of eight, individuals with mental handicaps that limit their accountability, translated beings from various dispensations, many of the billions to be born during the Millennium, and a significant percentage of those who receive the gospel in the spirit world—all these and more, according to what has been revealed, will be exalted through the great Plan of a merciful and loving Father in Heaven.

Although to some extent we have discussed how this is to be done on behalf of the aforementioned individuals, we have yet to address how you and I, living to adulthood in the dispensation of the fulness of times, yet have the odds for exaltation in our favor. Owing to the fact that we live in what is perceivably the last days before the second advent of Christ—and in a time filled with wickedness and temptations that seem unparalleled in the history of the world—one might wonder how a statistically high percentage of us will make it unscathed "through the fire," per se. Not surprisingly, this too the Lord has revealed.

On so many gospel subjects, the scriptures tend to present both sides of a singular gospel coin. For example, we read of the oneness of God (see John 10:30), but also of the individual nature of the three members of the Godhead (see Matthew 3:16–17). In one place we're told that there are but two churches—Christ's church and the devil's church (see 1 Nephi 14:10)—but elsewhere we read that all that is edifying is inspired of God (see Moroni 7:13). In some places we're taught of the importance of works (see James 2:14, 17–24, 26), and in other places we read of our dependency upon God's saving grace (see 2 Nephi 25:23; Romans 3:23–24). These are by no means contradictions. They are simply different facets of the same doctrinal diamond. Both aspects must be understood, believed, and practiced. None can be taken out of context. Each has its place in our divinely designed journey back to the Father and in our eventual exaltation in His kingdom.

Thus we turn our attention now to the doctrine of sanctification, the flip side, as it were, to the doctrine of justification. Traditionally, Latter-day Saints define justification as the divine declaration that one is righteous and innocent before God.[1] The *Encyclopedia of Mormonism* puts it this way: "Justification is a scriptural metaphor drawn from the courts of law: a judge justifies an accused person by declaring or pronouncing that person innocent. Likewise, God may treat a person as being 'not guilty' of sin."[2] In

Section 132 of the Doctrine and Covenants we read: "All covenants, contracts, bonds, obligations, oaths, vows, performances, connections, associations, or expectations, that are not made and entered into and sealed by the Holy Spirit of promise . . . are of no efficacy, virtue, or force in and after the resurrection from the dead; for all contracts that are not made unto this end have an end when men are dead" (v. 7). In other words, if one's ordinances are not sealed by the Holy Spirit of Promise, it is as though they did not happen. Baptism, confirmation, priesthood ordination, initiation, endowment, and sealing must each be sealed by the Holy Spirit of Promise in order to be salvific or efficacious. Receiving the ordinances is not enough. We must be worthy of them and be faithful to the covenants we make with the Lord in association with each of them. Elder Bruce R. McConkie taught:

> An act that is justified by the Spirit is one that is sealed by the Holy Spirit of Promise, or in other words, ratified and approved by the Holy Ghost. This law of justification is the provision the Lord has placed in the gospel to assure that no unrighteous performance will be binding on earth and in heaven, and that no person will add to his position or glory in the hereafter by gaining an unearned blessing.[3]

Basically the doctrine of justification is the declaration that we are "right" before God. It establishes that we are "acceptable" and "acquitted" of shortcomings, sins, and transgressions committed by us in our struggle to become like God and submit our will to Him. It is the validation or acceptance of the ordinances and covenants we have made or entered into. Justification is the saving imperative that balances the scales that we have tipped through our sins and failings. It is a blessing that only the three members of the Godhead can secure for us. The Father provides the Plan and its ordinances, the Son provides the Atonement to resolve our shortcomings, and the Holy Ghost ratifies our acts and ordinances via the parameters the Father has set and through the Atonement the Son has wrought. But no amount of effort on our part can accomplish this. No words confessed, no deeds done, no ordinances completed can secure it for us. Justification is an act of God. It is a gift given those who have sought, amid all their mortal imperfections, to be faithful to commandments and covenants. It is an act of grace, love, and mercy. Justification, or being "right" with God, is requisite for exaltation. But so also is sanctification.

Sanctification is the doctrinal principle that each of God's children must be made clean, holy, and set apart. Each must become a "saint."[4] Since no unclean thing can enter God's presence (see 3 Nephi 27:19), each of us—whether in an effort to have the companionship of a member of the Godhead during mortality or in an attempt to enter the celestial kingdom—must be changed incrementally to become like God and to be clean as God is. Whereas justification makes us "right" with God, sanctification makes us "clean" and "holy" before God.

Similar to justification, sanctification also comes through the Holy Spirit. Indeed, the scriptures indicate that it is the Holy Ghost, rather than the ordinance of baptism, that makes us "clean." It is the Holy Spirit that brings a remission of sins and allows us to access the atonement of the Lord Jesus Christ. Thus, to forfeit the Spirit is to forfeit forgiveness, redemption, and reconciliation. The scriptures are replete with declarations of the sanctifying or cleansing and changing power of the Holy Ghost. For example, in 2 Nephi 31:17 we read:

> Wherefore, do the things which I have told you I have seen that your Lord and your Redeemer should do; for, for this cause have they been shown unto me, that ye might know the gate by which ye should enter. For the gate by which ye should enter is repentance and baptism by water; and *then cometh a remission of your sins by fire and by the Holy Ghost.* (emphasis added)

Similarly, in 3 Nephi 27:20 we find this: "Now this is the commandment: Repent, all ye ends of the earth, and come unto me and be baptized in my name, that ye may *be sanctified by the reception of the Holy Ghost, that ye may stand spotless before me at the last day*" (emphasis added). Alma taught this: "Your brethren . . . humble themselves and do walk after the holy order of God, wherewith they have been brought into this church, *having been sanctified by the Holy Spirit,* and they do bring forth works which are meet for repentance" (Alma 5:54; emphasis added). Alma also taught: "Now they, after *being sanctified by the Holy Ghost,* having their garments made white, *being pure and spotless before God,* could not look upon sin save it were with abhorrence; and there were many, exceedingly great many, who were made pure and entered into the rest of the Lord their God" (Alma 13:12; emphasis added).

Similarly, the presiding brethren in this last dispensation have also described the role of the Holy Ghost in the repentance process. The Prophet Joseph Smith taught:

> You might as well baptize a bag of sand as a man, if not done in view of the remission of sins and getting of the Holy Ghost. Baptism by water is but half a baptism, and is good for nothing without the other half—that is, the baptism of the Holy Ghost . . . The baptism of water, without the baptism of fire and the Holy Ghost attending it, is of no use; they are necessarily and inseparably connected.[5]

Elder Bruce R. McConkie frequently spoke of this doctrine. Among other things, he wrote this: "Sins are remitted not in the waters of baptism, as we say in speaking figuratively, but when we receive the Holy Ghost."[6] In this same source he stated: "The Holy Ghost is a sanctifier; he alone, by divine appointment, has power to sanctify a human soul."[7] He also taught: "The actual cleansing of the soul comes when the Holy Ghost is received."[8] Elder Henry B. Eyring, then a member of the Quorum of the Twelve Apostles, stated:

> If you have felt the influence of the Holy Ghost during this day, or even this evening, you may take it as evidence that the Atonement is working in your life. For that reason . . . you would do well to put yourself in places and in tasks that invite the promptings of the Holy Ghost. Feeling the influence of the Holy Ghost . . . cleanses us through the Atonement of Jesus Christ.[9]

Elder D. Todd Christofferson, then of the presidency of the Seventy, wrote: "The Holy Spirit [is] the medium through whom atoning grace is applied to remit sins and sanctify souls."[10]

Thus, we understand that it is by our receipt of the Holy Ghost that the Atonement remits our sins. The Lord has established a number of ways in which this can happen in our lives. Certainly sincere repentance can bring manifestations of the Holy Spirit, as can something as simple as earnest prayer or focused scripture study.

Of course partaking of the sacrament serves as an opportunity for the baptized individual to renew covenants made at the waters of baptism and thereby receive anew the Holy Ghost's manifestation and sanctifying influence. To "renew" means to "make new again" or to "reenter" those covenants. When we partake of the sacrament we are renewing—or remaking—the covenants we entered into at baptism. When I was converted to The Church of Jesus Christ of Latter-day Saints at about 19 years of age, I certainly didn't understand this concept. I intentionally did not partake of the sacrament for many months after my baptism, not because of any grievous sins but because I knew that I wasn't perfect—and I didn't want to eat and drink damnation to my soul (see 3 Nephi 18:28–29). Later, while serving as a missionary, I had several elders point out how lucky they thought I was to be baptized at 19, as so many of the temptations of youth would have come and gone before my baptism. Again, naively, I believed that they were probably right! When an 84-year-old investigator of mine committed to baptism I remember thinking, *Now that's the way to do it! Live your whole life and then get baptized when your desire to sin has basically left you!* I clearly didn't understand the doctrine of sanctification, nor the Lord's expectations regarding our "perfection."

The language of the sacramental prayers emphasizes the relationship between the Holy Ghost and the remission of sins. The requirements and promises in the two sacramental prayers are very similar. For the sake of brevity, we will just examine the prayer offered over the bread.[11]

THE COVENANT ASSOCIATED WITH THE BREAD	COMMENTARY ON THE COVENANT
O God, the Eternal Father, we ask thee in the name of thy Son, Jesus Christ, to bless and sanctify this bread to the souls of all those who partake of it,	We request, not that the bread be sanctified, but rather that it have a sanctifying effect on those who partake of it.
that they may eat in remembrance of the body of thy Son,	We commit to think about what Christ has done for us.
and witness unto thee, O God, the Eternal Father, that they are willing to take upon them the name of thy Son, and always remember him and keep his commandments which he has given them;	We commit to being "WILLING" to keep the commandments, remember Christ, and live an exemplary life. There is nothing indicating perfection will be achieved in mortality. But we MUST be willing.
that they may always have his Spirit to be with them. Amen.	In return for all of this, we are promised that the Spirit (the "Sanctifier") will be with us (as long as we remain willing or desirous to keep God's commands).

As Elder McConkie put it: "And thus it is that we receive a remission of our sins through baptism and through the sacrament. The Spirit will not dwell in an unclean tabernacle, and when men receive the Spirit, they become clean and pure and spotless."[12]

Because of this sanctifying effect of the sacrament, I have always been somewhat uncomfortable when, at a baptismal service, people will say to the newly baptized person, "Now you're the cleanest person in this room." This implies that somehow the doctrine of sanctification—particularly as it relates to the ordinance of the sacrament—is inoperative in the lives of those attending the baptismal service.[13] Assuming each of us is sincerely striving to keep his or her covenants and regularly partaking of both the sacrament and the Holy Spirit, all of us are clean.

Another facet of the doctrine of sanctification is found in the words of James, the brother of Jesus. He wrote: "Is any sick among you? let him call for the elders of the church; and let them pray over him, anointing him with oil in the name of the Lord: And the prayer of faith shall save the sick, and the Lord shall raise him up; and if he have committed sins, they shall be forgiven him" (James 5:14–15). Here James informs us that, if we are healed physically through a priesthood blessing, we are also cleansed spiritually, as the Spirit of God is the primary moving force in healing those sick or afflicted—and the Holy Spirit will not dwell in an unclean tabernacle.

In discussions about the doctrine of sanctification, we are also wont to quote the Lord's words, when He declared: "Nevertheless, ye are blessed, for the testimony which ye have borne is recorded in heaven for the angels to look upon; and they rejoice over you, and your sins are forgiven you" (D&C 62:3; see also 84:61). By bearing your testimony when *truly* moved upon by the Holy Ghost, your sins are forgiven because speaking by the power of the Holy Spirit means that you have the Holy Spirit; and if you have the Spirit with you, you are clean and pure before the Lord.

Regarding this matter, Elder Bruce R. McConkie has said:

> The relationship between the bearing of testimony by the power of the Holy Ghost and the forgiveness of sins illustrates a glorious gospel truth. It is that whenever faithful Saints gain the companionship of the Holy Spirit they are clean and pure before the Lord, for the Spirit will not dwell in an unclean tabernacle. Hence, they thereby receive a remission of those sins committed after baptism. This same eternal verity is illustrated in the ordinance of administering to the sick. A faithful saint who is anointed with oil has the promise that "the prayer of faith shall save the sick, and the Lord shall raise him up; and if he have committed sins, they shall be forgiven him." (James 5:14–15.) The reasoning of the ancient apostle James, in this instance, is that since the miracle of healing comes by the power of the Holy Ghost, the sick person is healed not only physically but spiritually, for the Spirit who comes to heal will not dwell in a spiritually unclean tabernacle.[14]

All of this begs the question, How do we know if our sins have been remitted by the Holy Ghost? Of course there is the Lord's general counsel: "By this ye may know if a man repenteth of his sins—behold, he will confess them and forsake them" (D&C 58:43). But beyond that, it seems one of the easiest ways to know your standing before the Lord is to look for the Spirit's active and regular influence in your life. If you are frequently feeling, often being directed by, or consistently being prompted by the Holy Ghost, you are on the right path.

But then, one might logically ask, "How do I know if I have the Spirit with me? What does it feel like? How do I know if I am regularly being directed or influenced by it?" These are questions that only *you* can fully answer.

The scriptures do describe what one should feel when one has the Holy Spirit. For example, in Galatians 5:22–23 the apostle Paul tells us: "The fruit of the Spirit is love, joy, peace, longsuffering, gentleness, goodness, faith, meekness, [and] temperance." As the Lord's Spirit works upon us, changing us, so that we are more like God, we will feel many of these things. It should be noted, however, that these attributes are the result of the Spirit's influence on us—over time. It would be unreasonable to expect that the instant the gift of the Holy Ghost is bestowed upon us that we will immediately be completely loving, gentle, temperate, longsuffering, and so forth. Such attributes develop over time in one who is living a Spirit-directed life. Another indication of the Spirit's active influence in our life is described in Alma 19:33, where we are told that those whose "hearts had been changed" by the Holy Spirit "had no more desire to do evil." Similarly, Mosiah 5:2 informs us that "the Spirit of the Lord Omnipotent" can effect "a mighty change in us, or in our hearts, that we have no more disposition to do evil, but to do good continually." Again, such a change comes with time. These attributes do not appear the instant we encounter the Holy Ghost. Rather, as we grow in the Spirit, gaining a familiarity with how He speaks to us individually, honing our ability to follow those promptings, we will experience the promised change in our outlook and behavior.

Modern prophets have also given us instruction on how to recognize the Spirit's active influence in our life. After his martyrdom, the Prophet Joseph visited President Brigham Young. Among other things, he told him, "Tell the people to . . . be sure to keep the Spirit of the Lord and it will lead them right . . . They can tell the Spirit of the Lord from all other spirits; it will whisper peace and joy to their souls; it will take malice, hatred, strife and all evil from their hearts, and their whole desire will be to do good, bring forth righteousness, and build up the kingdom of God."[15]

The Spirit speaks in different ways to different people. No one description of how the influence of the Holy Ghost feels can be all inclusive. How He reveals to me and how He makes me feel may well be entirely different than how He speaks to you or how He influences you. But a significant factor in learning how to recognize that Spirit in your own life is to associate with it for a long enough period of time that you become accustomed to its consistent "feel" or "sound." And the best way to do that is to earnestly seek to live to the fullest of your ability all of the laws of the Lord. In addition, time spent in the Lord's holy house is one of the surest ways to gain a familiarity with the Lord's Spirit. Those who attend the temple regularly learn to recognize the promptings of the Holy Spirit.

In a masterful discourse on recognizing the influence of the Holy Spirit in our lives, Elder Jay E. Jensen of the Seventy described a number of ways in which the Spirit operates.[16] He noted that the Holy Ghost can speak peace to our minds (see D&C 6:23); it can cause our bosom to burn (see Luke 24:32); it can bring thoughts to our minds and feelings to our hearts (see D&C 8:2–3); it can cause an enlargement of our soul (see Alma 32:28); it sometimes comes as a voice to our minds (see Enos 1:10); it often leads us "to do good—yea, to do justly, to walk humbly, to judge righteously" (D&C 11:12); it can occupy our mind and press upon our feelings (see D&C 138:11); sometimes it constrains us (see Alma 14:11); when necessary, it will inspire others to help or intervene on our behalf (see D&C 1:38; 46:29); it can give us specific gifts, abilities, or knowledge (see D&C 46:9–29); and it can teach us and bring things to our remembrance (see John 14:26). These are but a few of the signs that the Holy Ghost is active in our life.

Now for a word or two on the subject of repentance. Our English word *repent* comes from the Greek word *metanoeo,* which means "to change your mind" or to "think differently." In other words, to "repent" does *not* mean that one completely stops sinning. Were such the true definition, no human being would be able to repent, as none of us have the ability to completely stop sinning. Rather, to "repent" means to begin to "think differently" about sin. So, for example, people who sin are unrepentant when they enjoy committing sin and wish down deep that the sinful acts they do were not prohibited by the Lord. Repentant people, on the other hand, are those who still occasionally commit sins but deeply desire to overcome their fallen and sinful natures. They love the commandments, are desirous to comply with the Lord's will, and loathe sin in all of its forms. Thus, the difference between repentant and unrepentant is not sinless verses sinful. Rather, it is the difference between the desire to be good and the desire that the commandments be rescinded. What's striking is that the Lord asks us to "repent," or "think differently" about sin, if we wish salvation. He asks us to learn to think as He thinks about sin and unrighteousness. He does not, however, tell us that we must never sin again if we are to be saved. What He asks of us in this regard is entirely within the realm of human possibility. We *can* change our thoughts, desires, and attitudes. Of course, as with all else spiritual, we must rely upon Him and His Holy Spirit to bring to pass this "mighty change" in us (Mosiah 5:2; Alma 5:12–14). But it can be done.

Certainly none of us should ever be cavalier about repentance. Note this warning by the Prophet Joseph: "Repentance is a thing that cannot be trifled with every day. Daily transgression and daily repentance is not that which is pleasing in the sight of God."[17] Sins that we struggle with day in and day out require our sincere and focused attention. Indeed, in some cases they may require the involvement of a priesthood leader, such as a bishop or stake president. When we choose to do things that make it impossible for the Holy Ghost to stay with us, we forfeit the Spirit's companionship and place ourselves—at least for a time—beyond the reach of the atonement of the Lord Jesus Christ. Contingent upon what we've done wrong, sometimes getting the Spirit's companionship back can be difficult. Hence the Prophet's warning to not "trifle" with sin and feigned repentance.

Nonetheless, the doctrine of sanctification is evidence of how very simple it is to ensure our exaltation. If one but keeps the Spirit, he or she will be clean and therefore saved! *It is that simple!* All other requirements will come naturally. Indeed, the companionship of the Holy Ghost will change our natures in such a way that we will no longer desire to do evil. Instead, He will create in us a desire to do good continually (see Alma 19:33). Regarding the doctrine of sanctification, President Brigham Young once remarked:

> If a person with an honest heart, a broken, contrite, and pure spirit, in all fervency and honesty of soul, presents himself and says that he wishes to be baptized for the remission of his sins, and the ordinance is administered by one having authority, is that man saved? Yes, to that period of time. Should the Lord see proper to take him then from the earth, the man has believed and been baptized, and is a fit subject for heaven—a candidate for the kingdom of God in the celestial world, because he has repented and done all that was required of him to that hour. . . . It is present salvation and the present influence of the Holy Ghost that we need every day to keep us on saving ground. When an individual . . . continue[s] in righteousness and obedience to the requirements of heaven, he is saved all the time, through baptism, the laying on of hands, and obeying the commandments of the Lord and all that is required of him by the heavens—the living oracles. He is saved now, next week, next

> year, and continually, and is prepared for the celestial kingdom of God whenever the time comes for him to inherit it.[18]

It has been said: "To the saints the continual cry of the gospel is: *Sanctify yourselves.* (D&C 39:18; 43:9, 11, 16; 133:4; Leviticus 11:44; 1 Pet. 1:15)."[19] Why is such the case? Because for those of us who have been given the blessing from God to live to the age of maturity upon this telestial earth, retention of the Holy Ghost is the key to our exaltation. Each of us knows what things chase the Spirit from our lives. We know what things the Brethren have in wisdom counseled us to avoid—to prohibit from entering into our lives and hearts. If we are honest with ourselves and with the Lord then the task of seeking exaltation will be an easy one. A number of years ago Elder J. Richard Clarke of the Seventy stated: "Most damage to the collective reputation of the Church is done by those members who want to straddle the line, with one foot in the kingdom and the other foot in spiritual Babylon. Those who so compromise their principles want to play for both teams at once—the Lord's and Satan's."[20] Such is also the case with the individual soul.

Those who seek to straddle the fence—who seek to have one foot in Zion (for safety) and one foot in Babylon (for fun)—find themselves constantly overwhelmed with temptations and guilt. They constantly question the apostle Paul's prophetic promise that God never allows us to be tempted beyond our ability to withstand (see 1 Corinthians 10:13), forgetting that Paul's promise is conditioned upon our sincere efforts to avoid temptation and stay connected with God's Holy Spirit. Sanctification, cleansing, and change come to those who seek to keep the Holy Spirit as their guide and companion. But if we think we can have both Zion and Babylon as our home, we fool ourselves, and we make our celestial pursuit an impossible dream.

The path to exaltation was designed by our Father in Heaven to be a reasonably easy one. The way has been clearly laid out. Modern prophets and apostles regularly warn us of pitfalls and dangers. Uncomfortable or unpleasant feelings naturally well up in us when we choose wrong over right, thereby warning us to return to the path of safety and true happiness. And the Spirit has been offered to us as a constant companion so that we needn't walk the path alone. Yet, amid all of this constant reinforcement, some of us consciously choose to make things more difficult than they need to be, simply by ignoring what has been given and thereby willingly forfeiting the protection, guidance, and sanctification that comes through God's Holy Spirit.

The way is *so* very simple. The odds are in our favor. All we need do is stick with the Spirit. Again, from one of the Lord's anointed, Elder Bruce R. McConkie, we read: "Whenever faithful saints gain the companionship of the Holy Spirit they are clean and pure before the Lord, for the Spirit will not dwell in an unclean tabernacle. Hence, they thereby receive a remission of those sins committed after baptism."[21]

A Spirit-directed Saint is a clean Saint, and a clean Saint is an exalted Saint! May we always seek to have His Spirit with us (see Moroni 4:3; 5:2; D&C 20:77–79; 1 Thessalonians 5:19).

CHAPTER FOUR

Vicarious Work for the Dead

One might rightfully ask: "What is the most important event in the history of the world?" I assume that every faithful Christian would reply something to the effect, "The infinite atonement of the Lord Jesus Christ." And rightfully so! But what of this question: "What is the second most important event in the history of the world?" Faithful Latter-day Saints necessarily must respond: "The First Vision and subsequent restoration of the fulness of the gospel."

But why? Why is the Restoration so close in significance to the Atonement as to justify its "second place" in the heavenly hierarchy of sacred events? In what sense is it second only to the atoning sacrifice of the Lord Jesus Christ? For clarification we turn our attention to the fiftieth chapter of the book of Genesis. Of the Prophet Joseph Smith, the Lord stated: "And that seer will I bless, . . . and his name shall be called Joseph, and it shall be after the name of his father; and he shall be like unto [Moses]; *for the thing which the Lord shall bring forth by his hand shall bring my people unto salvation*" (JST Genesis 50:33; emphasis added). Here we learn from the Lord's own lips that the things to be revealed through the Prophet Joseph Smith would be instrumental in bringing salvation to God's people!

Although it is seldom a point of emphasis in the Church, nonetheless, the fact of the matter is that access to and the efficacy of the Atonement—for most people who have ever lived upon this earth—is dependent upon the restoration of the fulness of the gospel through the Prophet Joseph. Think of it! Salvific ordinances have not been on the earth during the vast majority of its history. Certainly most people who have lived upon this planet have done so during a time or in a location where the full range of saving ordinances and doctrines were not available. During the days or years of their mortal probation, they lived unaware of the need for baptism, the sanctifying power in the gift of the Holy Ghost, the holy temple endowment, or the ordinance of celestial marriage. In the latter-day restoration of the gospel, these saving ordinances, which had been lost during the Apostasy, along with the practice of vicarious work for the dead, were returned to earth, so that *all* can have access to these necessary and exalting elements.

Were it not for the receptivity and courage of the Prophet Joseph, these necessary ordinances and gifts would not be available to the majority of God's children—not those living upon the earth now, nor most who lived in ages past. This understanding makes sense of the Lord's explanation of why He chose to reveal anew Himself along with the principles and ordinances of His gospel in these latter days:

> Wherefore, I the Lord, knowing the calamity which should come upon the inhabitants of the earth, called upon my servant Joseph Smith, Jun., and spake unto him from heaven, and gave him commandments;
>
> And also gave commandments to others, that they should proclaim these things unto the world; and all this that it might be fulfilled, which was written by the prophets—
>
> The weak things of the world shall come forth and break down the mighty and strong ones, that man should not counsel his fellow man, neither trust in the arm of flesh—
>
> But that every man might speak in the name of God the Lord, even the Savior of the world;
>
> That faith also might increase in the earth;
>
> That mine everlasting covenant might be established;
>
> That the fulness of my gospel might be proclaimed by the weak and the simple unto the ends of the world. (D&C 1:17–23)

In his initial visit to the then seventeen-year-old Joseph, Moroni declared: *"Behold, I will reveal unto you the Priesthood, by the hand of Elijah the prophet, before the coming of the great and dreadful day of the Lord. . . . And he shall plant in the hearts of the children the promises made to the fathers, and the hearts of the children shall turn to their fathers. If it were not so, the whole earth would be utterly wasted at his coming"* (JS–H 1:38–39). The simple truth is, were it not for the restoration of the gospel and its priesthood ordinances, when Christ returns—and at the final judgment—the majority of God's children would be without the saving ordinances required for their exaltation. Thus, Malachi informs us, the earth (which was created for the purpose of bringing salvation to the family of man) would have been "utterly wasted" (created in vain) and its inhabitants would be destroyed.[1]

As history has borne out, the Prophet Joseph endured much in the way of trials and persecution that the saving ordinances might be available to all.[2] Is it any wonder then that the Doctrine and Covenants declares of him: "Joseph Smith, the Prophet and Seer of the Lord, has done more, save Jesus only, for the salvation of men in this world, than any other man that ever lived in it," and that having done so, "sealed his mission and his works with his own blood" (D&C 135:3).

Christians who are not of our faith are so often offended by this statement. Indeed, one text criticized the Prophet Joseph Smith, claiming that the passage proved that he was boastful—the authors of the criticism apparently unaware that the Prophet did not write these words of himself.[3] Another author, offended by the doctrine taught in D&C 135:3, wrote: "The Mormons thank God for Joseph Smith, who claimed that he had done more for us than any other man, *including Jesus Christ.*"[4] (The calculation and blatancy of this misquotation is shocking!) If these critics understood the truth—*and in context*—they would see that the declaration of Joseph Smith's part in the salvation of mankind is not a blasphemous teaching! Nor is it a representation of Joseph's arrogance or of Mormonism's exclusivity. On the contrary, D&C 135:3 is simply proof that the God we worship is full of grace, love, mercy, and foresight. It is a powerful declaration that He is in fact "no respecter of persons" (Acts 10:34) and proof that God's great plan of happiness provides salvation for *all* men (see 1 Nephi 10:18; 2 Nephi 2:9–10)—not just the living, but also the dead; not just the Christians, but all of His children; not just the Mormons, but everyone!

In the words of Elder Neal A. Maxwell, "[The doctrine of] salvation for the dead" is "the means of insuring and demonstrating the mercy and justice of God."[5]

Of course there is always the danger that when we emphasize the greatness of the Plan, as created by the Father and revealed anew through His Prophet, Joseph, some will assume we are criticizing them or their faith. Nothing could be further from the truth. We are simply acknowledging that God is infinitely fair in His treatment of His children and that He has created a "contingency plan," as it were, for all those who do not have the opportunity to learn of, accept, follow, or obey Christ during their mortal probation. How could a just God damn someone for not accepting that which they did not know?

Somehow, so many who profess a belief in Christ's words and love, don't quite "get" this foundational Christian principle. Many years ago, while living in Europe, I had a conversation with a man that left me somewhat shocked. He stated to me that—and I in no way exaggerate the interchange—"all you need to do in order to be saved is to ask Jesus into your heart as your personal Lord and Savior and you are guaranteed you will go to heaven—you're saved!"

I asked him, "What of those who have never heard of Jesus or who know nothing about Him? What happens to them?"

He said, "They will go to hell."

"But they didn't know," I insisted, "so how could a just God damn them for what they did not know?"

And here is what "knocked my socks off": He replied, "If they were sincere, good people, they would find a way to learn the truth about what they don't know. That's why they deserve to go to hell!"

What I said next can only be explained by my total amazement at his declaration. I said to the man, "Guess what I'm thinking."

He replied, "I don't follow. What do you mean?"

Again I said, "Guess what I'm thinking—and if you can't guess it, you have to go to hell!"

He looked at me rather shocked, and then I said, "This seems to me to be the logic of what you're saying. You're basically claiming that God is telling the vast majority of the world that if they can't guess the 'secret word,' they're going to be destroyed! The God I love and worship wants to save His children, not damn them. And He certainly would never act so unjustly as to send someone to hell for something He never allowed that person to know."[6]

The exchange reminded me a bit of the Zoromites and their arrogant prayer, which they offered while standing upon the Rameumptom. Among other things, they would pray: "Holy, holy

God; we believe that thou . . . hast elected us to be thy holy children; and also thou hast . . . elected us that we shall be saved, whilst all around us are elected to be cast by thy wrath down to hell; . . . And again we thank thee, O God, that we are a chosen and a holy people. Amen" (Alma 31:15–18). That was a self-righteous and pernicious doctrine then and would be so today.

Our attitude toward our non-LDS brothers and sisters should never be one of condescension or a secret desire for their damnation. On the contrary, we should pray for, hope for, and work for the salvation of *all* of God's children—even those who treat us as enemies (see Matthew 5:44). At the dedication of the Kirtland Temple in 1836, the Prophet Joseph included in his dedicatory prayer, given to him by revelation, these sentiments: "O Lord, we delight not in the destruction of our fellow men; their souls are precious before thee; . . . Have mercy, O Lord, upon the wicked mob, who have driven thy people, that they may cease to spoil, that they may repent of their sins if repentance is to be found" (D&C 109:43, 50).

One of the most beautiful tenets of the restored gospel of Jesus Christ is the merciful truth that God's Plan can and will save *all* who desire to return to His presence. No one person or class of people will be damned based on their lack of opportunity to join the Church or accept Christ during their mortal sojourns. Just as no one will be held accountable for another's sins or transgressions, no one will be punished or deprived for not doing something they simply didn't know they should do. And no one will be robbed of the opportunity to comply with God's laws and receive the blessings and ordinances prior to that great and final day of judgment. The Plan is perfectly fair and equitable! Each individual *will* have his or her chance!

After receiving a vision in the Kirtland Temple, in January of 1836, the Prophet Joseph testified:

> Thus came the voice of the Lord unto me, saying: All who have died without a knowledge of this gospel, who would have received it if they had been permitted to tarry, shall be heirs of the celestial kingdom of God; Also all that shall die henceforth without a knowledge of it, who would have received it with all their hearts, shall be heirs of that kingdom; For I, the Lord, will judge all men according to their works, according to the desire of their hearts. (D&C 137:7–9)

What a profound and glorious promise. What a comforting assurance given us by a God who cannot lie (see Titus 1:2)! How could anyone claiming faith in the Lord Jesus Christ see it any other way? The ordinances to be had in the holy temple—in concert with the life, ministry, atoning sacrifice, and resurrection of the Lord Jesus Christ—hold the answers to the woes and perplexities of all nations and of all peoples. The good, albeit confused, man I mentioned earlier was missing this significant piece of the "gospel puzzle"—and for that reason misunderstood God's manner of dealing with mankind. Had he understood the merciful principle of vicarious work for the dead, he too would have seen the Lord, not as a reticent Redeemer, but rather as a generous and willing Savior of souls!

Both the Bible[7] and the early Church fathers[8] taught that those who died without having had a chance to hear and accept the gospel would go to a place where, before they were resurrected, they would have a chance to be taught the truth about Christ, His atonement, and the purpose of life. The preaching of the gospel to receptive spirits who have departed this life—coupled with vicarious baptisms,[9] confirmations, ordinations, endowments, and sealings—makes it possible for those who did not have access to Christianity in its fulness to reap the full blessings of what God has in store for those who love Him, which blessings Paul said were impossible to imagine (see 1 Corinthians 2:9).

That those who departed this life without the benefit of having been taught the gospel would be provided for was confirmed in the revelation given to President Joseph F. Smith on October 3, 1918, after the prophet had been pondering "the great atoning sacrifice that was made by the Son of God, for the redemption of the world; And the great and wonderful love made manifest by the Father and the Son in the coming of the Redeemer into the world; That through his atonement, and by obedience to the principles of the gospel, mankind might be saved" (D&C 138:2–4). President Smith saw "the hosts of the dead, both small and great . . . [and] that they were filled with joy and gladness, and were rejoicing together because the day of their deliverance was at hand" (D&C 138:11, 15). God, who is merciful and kind, had provided for their redemption, though they had not been blessed to receive the gospel during mortality.

But why Joseph Smith over Paul or Moses or Nephi? For what reason is Joseph placed second only to Jesus when it comes to the scope of his work and the significance of his ministry? No doubt his valiancy in the premortal world played a significant role. Certainly his extraordinary gifts as a revelator and as a teacher of divine principles was a factor. But neither of these provide the full explanation of Joseph's stature and status before God.

A major reason Joseph's work weighs so heavily in the eternal scheme of things is the restoration of work for the dead that was revealed to him. It will be remembered that in Old Testament times no vicarious saving work for the dead was performed. Indeed, it was not until after Christ's resurrection that the first vicarious ordinances on behalf of the deceased were authorized.[10] And because of the first-century apostasy, work for the dead in the meridian of time only lasted for a very short time. Thus, all those who lived outside the covenant during the thousands of years that comprise the Old Testament era, and nearly all with the same status in the two thousand years since Christ's atonement, have been awaiting the Restoration through the Prophet Joseph, that their saving ordinances might be performed. We suppose those noncovenant peoples of the Old Testament patiently awaited the preaching of the gospel in the spirit world—which did not happen until Christ's own death, when He Himself initiated it (see 1 Peter 4:6). And we also assume those who have lived without the gospel light throughout the history of the world have just as patiently awaited the restoration of vicarious work for the dead—that all that they have been taught, and all which they have accepted in the spirit world, might be made valid as the efficacious ordinances are performed for them here upon the earth in the Lord's holy houses—the temples of the Living God. Heavenly Father designed it to be such. And Joseph was authorized to and succeeded in carrying it out, to the joy of untold billions who will be the recipients of that sacred service.

And so we come full circle. We began this chapter with the frank acknowledgment that "Mormonism," so called, admits Joseph Smith's significant role in making accessible Christ's atonement to the masses. Truly the preaching of the gospel to the receptive residing in the spirit world, coupled with vicarious saving ordinances performed on their behalf, is how all of this is to be accomplished. Once again, so, so many of God's children will be exalted—all because the Plan was designed in such a way to ensure their access to its exalting truths and ordinances. As we have already stated, the vast majority of all people who hear and accept the gospel of Jesus Christ (and its essential ordinances) will do so as residents of the spirit world, not as residents of this earth. Thanks be to God for making this contingency part of His Plan. Thanks be to Christ for working out the Atonement necessary that these ordinances would have meaning and power. And thanks be to the Prophet Joseph for being the instrument through which these glorious truths were restored and made accessible.

CHAPTER FIVE

WHAT OF THE "STRAIT AND NARROW PATH"?

Near the conclusion of His Sermon on the Mount, the Lord declared: "Enter ye in at the strait gate: for wide is the gate, and broad is the way, that leadeth to destruction, and many there be which go in thereat: Because strait is the gate, and narrow is the way, which leadeth unto life, and few there be that find it" (Matthew 7:13–14; see also 3 Nephi 14:13–14; 27:33). Naturally, one cannot help but wonder how this declaration squares with all we have been saying. How can one remain optimistic regarding the odds of their exaltation when this divine declaration *seems* to imply that "few" will find their way back to the Father? The answer to these questions is to be found in the context of the Lord's words.

General Authorities and Latter-day Saint scholars alike have noted that Jesus' words regarding the "strait and narrow path" must be taken in context of the entire plan of salvation.[1] Clearly Jesus *isn't* directing this warning to those who have died prior to the age of accountability—and, as we have shown, that is an enormous number of God's children. *Nor* are His words here directed to those who live life under the cloud of a mental disability, which limits their accountability during this mortal probation. Jesus was *not* addressing His caution to those who will receive the gospel in the spirit world, because they had no chance to receive it in mortality (which is the case for the vast majority of *all* people who live to the age of accountability). Thus, this *seemingly* sad statistic *does not* apply to the vast majority of Father's children.[2] So, for whom was this admonition or warning intended?

We know that the gate to which Jesus referred is repentance and baptism (see 2 Nephi 31:17–19). But baptism is only the gate to the *path,* which leads to exaltation; it is not the gate to the celestial kingdom itself. LDS scholars D. Kelly Ogden and Andrew C. Skinner put it this way: "Baptism is not the door to our heavenly mansion but the gate to the path that leads to the mansion."[3] Elder Bruce R. McConkie wrote: "Baptism is the strait gate which puts men on the path leading to the celestial world; the new and everlasting covenant of marriage is the strait gate which starts men and women out in the direction of exaltation in the highest heaven of that world."[4] Thus, there is much to be done once we pass through that gate and begin our travels upon the path. Once on that course we must press forward (see 1 Nephi 8:24) until—through a combination of our efforts and Christ's atonement—we obtain a place in the highest degree of the celestial kingdom of our God.

This being the case, it may well be that Jesus is speaking to that very small and select group of individuals who encounter the fulness of the gospel in mortality, prayerfully receive a confirming witness that it is true, and are confronted with the question, "Should I join or not?" It is to these that the Lord's command has meaning and provokes accountability. For all others it is impossible to obey the command to "enter ye in at the strait gate," as they will only be introduced to that gate in the spirit world after accepting the gospel message and a vicarious baptism for the dead. Thus, a colleague of mine is wont to say: "Strait is the gate, and narrow is the way, and few there be that find it IN THIS LIFE."[5]

This, I think, is demonstrated in the prophet Lehi's vision of the tree of life (see 1 Nephi 8), which seems to focus on this small, select group of Heavenly Father's children who have encountered the gate and are thereby confronted with a decision as to what they should (or will) do. The vision depicts individuals who have a knowledge of—and perhaps even a witness of—the gospel of Jesus Christ; and yet each is at a crossroads where they must decide whether they will enter the path and pursue the ultimate goal being offered—namely, exaltation in the celestial kingdom.

Though the vision offers a detailed discussion about what the various individuals do who have decided to enter the path (i.e., who have chosen to join the Lord's Church by entering into the covenant of baptism), nevertheless, the intriguing symbol in this vision—as it relates to our discussion—would be Laman and Lemuel.

Lehi tells us that the fruit of the "was desirable to make one happy" (v. 10). He says that it is "sweet, above all that [he had] ever before tasted" (v. 11), and that partaking of it "filled [his] soul with exceedingly great joy" (v. 12), so much so that he was "desirous that [his] family should partake of it also" (v. 12). He notes:

> And as I cast my eyes round about, that perhaps I might discover my family also, I beheld a river of water; and it ran along, and it was near the tree of which I was partaking the fruit. And I looked to behold . . . at the head thereof I beheld your mother Sariah, and Sam, and Nephi; and they stood as if they knew not whither they should go. And it came to pass that I beckoned unto them; and I also did say unto them with a loud voice that they should come unto me, and partake of the fruit, which was desirable above all other fruit. And it came to pass that they did come unto me and partake of the fruit also. And it came to pass that I was desirous that Laman and Lemuel should come and partake of the fruit also; wherefore, I cast mine eyes towards the head of the river, that perhaps I might see them. And it came to pass that I saw them, but they would not come unto me and partake of the fruit. (1 Nephi 8:13–18)

In the vision, all who discovered the path—who found the Church and gospel of Jesus Christ—were offered an opportunity of pursuing a course that ultimately leads to eternal life. However, as the vision shows us, not all who encounter the path will accept it or choose to enter its gate through accepting the ordinance and covenant of baptism. Laman and Lemuel are prime examples of those who, when confronted with the question, "Should I join or not?" make the decision to abstain, simply because of "the fear of persecution and the cares of the world" overwhelm them and cause them "to reject the word" (D&C 40:2). It is to individuals such as these that the Lord's command to "enter ye in at the strait gate" has meaning and provokes accountability. It is a command to the very few who, while as mortals, learn of the gospel and have to make the difficult and life-changing decisions "Should I join?" and "Can I live the lifestyle God's Spirit is calling me to live?"

It is true that *in mortality* only a relative few will find and accept the gospel, and, as Lehi's vision suggests, all who are baptized will not necessarily reach the prize. But if you are a faithful member of the Church who has willingly set aside the enticements of a fallen world to enter into covenants that you are striving to keep, then odds are you're going to realize the promises made to you, and you will be exalted.

Speaking in general terms, what constitutes rejecting Christ and His gospel in mortality? Certainly one must have sufficient knowledge to make one accountable. Indeed, Elder McConkie indicated that Jesus was "speaking to accountable persons and of attainment of the celestial kingdom."[6] He was not speaking to those without a witness of the restored gospel and its ordinances. Of course one is not accountable until one has the opportunity to know the gospel is true. And what constitutes an opportunity? Being taught by an authorized representative, feeling the Spirit, recognizing the Spirit, and then rejecting that witness when you know it is telling you the Church is true.[7]

We may occasionally (I think naively so) assume that someone is accountable, simply because they have had interactions with members of the Church—or even with missionaries—when, in reality, they are not accountable. Permit me to illustrate with a personal experience.

In the mid-1980s, I was serving as a full-time missionary in the south of Great Britain. On a particular day my companion and I were knocking doors in a neighborhood where many people were home. We knew they were home, not because they were answering their doors, but, rather, because we could see them as we passed their windows. Yet few were willing to answer their doors when we knocked. Both my companion and I began to feel a bit frustrated that so many of the people living in that neighborhood would neither listen to our message nor be so courteous as to acknowledge us at the door. After knocking on several doors where we knew for sure the occupants where home, and yet none had answered, my companion bent down and announced through the mail slot in the door, "We're the Mormons!" I was puzzled by his behavior but didn't ask about it until he had done it again at the next two doors. I asked, "Elder, why are you doing that?"

He replied, "I'm making them accountable."

I said, "You're what?!?"

Again, he said, "I'm making them accountable." To which I replied, "If that's all it takes to make someone accountable, the Church could just run one international commercial for about a week and send everyone to hell!"

Perhaps I should have asked why he would want to make those who hadn't heard his message accountable, as that doesn't seem like the way the Lord works. Though it certainly is not our place to judge who is and who isn't accountable, nonetheless, I think it is fair to say that the Lord does not condemn those who do not know. And in the case of His teachings about the "strait and narrow path," those who do not know are not the ones He is addressing.[8]

Of the question as to what Christ meant by His declaration: "Wide is the gate, and broad is the way, that leadeth to destruction, and many there be which go in thereat: Because strait is the gate, and narrow is the way, which leadeth unto life, and few there be that find it," Elder Bruce R. McConkie stated: "The scriptures speak often of a strait and narrow path that leads to eternal life, and stress is frequently placed on the fact that few of the sons and daughters of God will find their way to the end of that path. But these are scriptural passages that must be viewed in proper perspective."[9] And what is that "proper perspective"?

As noted above, it is the recognition that this is not a comment about the vast majority of individuals who will dwell upon this earth. Rather, Christ's words are clearly directed to a very small handful who will have the privilege of coming into contact with the fulness of the gospel during their mortal probations. Simply put, not many will make it onto that path *in mortality,* relative to how many make it in the spirit world. And why is that the case? Because so few mortals will have the chance of learning of the fulness of the gospel during mortality. But the vast majority of all of God's children will make it back! They will be saved! They will be exalted! As Elder McConkie put it: "Truly, in the aggregate, there are many who shall be saved!"[10]

This innumerable host will be saved because, like you and I, who have felt the Spirit and know the gospel to be true, most who hear it in the spirit world will also feel the Holy Ghost testifying to them that the restored gospel is right and true and will therefore willingly join—rejoicing at having finally found the path that eluded them during mortality.

The four-volume *Doctrinal Commentary on the Book of Mormon* expresses it this way: "In the long run, we must ever keep in mind that our God and Father is a successful parent, one who will save far more of his children than he will lose! . . . Indeed, who can count the number of saved beings in eternity? Our God, who is triumphant in all battles against the forces of evil, will surely be victorious in the numbers of his children who will be saved."[11] Joseph Fielding McConkie wrote this: "Of those who kept their first estate and gained the privilege of being born into mortality the vast majority will return to the presence of their heavenly parents to receive the fulness of their divine inheritance. . . . The great victory in numbers will be the Lord's . . . that he will save (meaning exalt) the greater portion of his children."[12]

Yes, the Lord spoke rightly when He said, "Broad is the way" that leads "to destruction." But this declaration only serves to remind us that in a world of "anything goes" there are many dangers and pitfalls we must be aware of and avoid. While the Lord is clearly *not* saying most of His children end up following the path that leads to destruction, He *does* appear to be warning us that hard choices will have to be made by all—and particularly by those who are blessed to be led to the fulness of His gospel while they are yet participating in the mortal experience. However, His warnings (through prophets and apostles—ancient and modern) of the dangers of the "broad way" only serve to show how much He loves us and how much He will do to ensure that all who wish to be saved will have sufficient direction to recognize and avoid the path that leads to eternal damnation.

As optimistic as all of this seems, some may feel that the scales seem a bit unbalanced. So many, having died before the age of accountability or having the promise that they will be born during the Millennium, have or will seemingly be spared the tests and trials you and I are going through. How can we be judged with them, when their accountability and their test seems so much less than ours? Has God's mercy toward some robbed you and me of the justice we naturally feel we deserve? Such cannot be the case, for were it so, God would cease to be God! It must be remembered that those blessed to have an extended mortal experience have many opportunities that those who die prematurely envy. We are privileged to enjoy a plethora of experiences which provide meaningful and profound learning and growth. We are given the chance to develop and utilize divine gifts and talents. We have opportunities to serve in the kingdom in significant ways, influencing the lives of others, and reaping the blessings that come through that service. And we are blessed to enter into and nurture relationships that will extend beyond the veil. Indeed, all these—and a thousand other advantages—place you and me in an enviable position in the minds of those who were not blessed to live a full and long life upon this earth. The "few" from our day who will find the path are not an imbalanced or unfair statistic. Indeed, we who have a knowledge of the gospel and its covenants have advantages over those who traverse the mortal experience without the divine understanding. It is often said, "For of him unto whom much is given much is required" (D&C 82:3). However, the inverse is also true: where more is expected of us, more blessings are provided to us. We are not in the dark as to the purpose of life, the requirements for salvation, or the dangers of mortality, as the vast majority of the inhabitants of this earth are and have been. Additionally, we within the covenant have been sent at this time in the world's history to do what God the Father needs us to do and what He has equipped us to do.

Although this may sound arrogant, such is not the case. No spirit of exclusivity, racism, derogation, or denigration is intended or implied.[13] The scriptures are quite clear: God works through His covenant people—whether Israel of antiquity, the Christians of the common era, or the Mormons of modernity. Those who in mortality have entered into and striven to keep the restored covenants of the fulness of the gospel of Jesus Christ were foreordained to do so in the grand council before the world was.[14] It is no coincidence that they have been born with, or have had access to, the truths of the Restoration. This was by divine design. It was the will of God. It is the plan of God. Those who seek out, find, and embrace the fulness of the gospel in mortality are the sheep who hear and respond to Christ's voice (see John 10:27). They have "believing blood."[15] And in many cases they enjoy greater spiritual endowments than those outside of the covenant.[16] For these reasons God is able to use them to bring to pass His latter-day work. And for these reasons God also equips them and blesses them beyond measure—that they might do what He wills by living as He asks. Of course, their agency is ever preserved; and it is for this reason that there are "few" of them who during mortality find the path. As one commentary notes: "Relatively few are genuinely interested in entering the gate and walking that path"[17]—although all these of which we speak are endowed with the necessary drive and ability to succeed, if they desire to do so. That is part of the promised blessing. It has been said: "Once a person enters through the gospel gate, in turnstile fashion, his life is different. As time passes he finds there are fewer and fewer things he can do in the world and still retain the influence and guidance of the Holy Spirit. At first, such seems restrictive but in time he begins to feel and sense the liberating power which flows from Christ to him through the covenants and ordinances of the gospel. What at first may have been viewed as an infringement on his liberties is now seen to be the very key to personal freedom and peace. He has come to know the Lord, who is the Truth, and the Truth has made him free (see John 8:31–32)."[18]

Thus, yes, "narrow is the way" that leads to exaltation. And true it is, few mortals get to enter the gate to exaltation during their earthly probation. But we have the assurance of modern prophets and apostles that the total number of those who will be lost—the total from the spirit world and mortality combined—is small, very small indeed.[19] And, as a protection to those whom God will place upon the path in mortality, great spiritual endowments are made available to those who seek them.[20] Their mortal experience is not that of their non-covenant brothers and sisters. And though all things are equal in the economy of God, the heightened access to the fulness of God's blessings provided those upon the path will, in the eternities, make all things equal in the minds of those who were required to make the journey here![21]

CHAPTER SIX

WHEN A LOVED ONE STRAYS

These are trying times in which we live. The temptations to which each of us is exposed—youth and adult alike—are in frequency and intensity beyond anything imagined in times past. Lascivious movies, music, and moral relativism are rampant, sending confusing messages to impressionable minds and spirits. Having a strong testimony of the gospel of Jesus Christ has never been more important than it is today. Indeed, even in his day, President Heber C. Kimball warned:

> To meet the difficulties that are coming, it will be necessary for you to have a knowledge of the truth of this work for yourselves. The difficulties will be of such a character that the man or woman who does not possess this personal knowledge or witness will fall. If you have not got the testimony, live right and call upon the Lord and cease not till you obtain it. If you do not you will not stand. Remember these sayings . . . The time will come when no man nor woman

> will be able to endure on borrowed light. Each will have to be guided by the light within himself. If you do not have it, how can you stand?[1]

This era is certainly among the times President Kimball prophetically envisioned. Those not firmly grounded in the gospel—those without strong testimonies—will, in the words of the apostle Paul, be "tossed to and fro, and carried about with every wind of doctrine, by the sleight of men, and cunning craftiness, whereby they lie in wait to deceive" (Ephesians 4:14). Metaphorically speaking, weak and unspiritual members are rudderless and destined to be dashed against the jagged rocks of mortal temptations.

Those with eyes wide open cannot help but feel some degree of concern over that which is taking place in the world around us today. Having said that, President Gordon B. Hinckley—an eternal optimist—time and again addressed the dangers of pessimism. Among other things, he said:

> I stand here today as an optimist . . . I realize, of course, that we are beset with many tragic problems. . . . I have seen a good deal of this earth. I have seen its rot and smelled its filth. I have been in areas where war rages and hate smolders in the hearts of people. I have seen the appalling poverty that hovers over many lands. I have seen the oppression of those in bondage and the brutality of their overlords . . . I have watched with alarm the crumbling morals of our society.

> And yet I am an optimist. I have a simple and solemn faith that right will triumph and that truth will prevail.[2]

With all that may seem wrong in the world, there is so much of good. Indeed, according to President Hinckley, "This is the greatest age in the history of the earth . . . We have every reason to be optimistic."[3] Satan may use things, such as the media, to his advantage. But the Lord also uses it to move forth the gospel in a marvelous manner unimagined fifty years ago. President Hinckley mused, "I do not know how anybody can feel gloomy for very long who is a member of this Church."[4] He also wisely noted: "Looking at the dark side of things always leads to a spirit of pessimism which so often leads to defeat."[5] "We have a great message to give to the world, a message of hope, a message of assurance that all is not lost."[6] There is no place for pessimism among faithful Latter-day Saints, and that includes pessimism about their chance for gaining exaltation. God has created a plan—a plan that works! Too many go about claiming they have a testimony of the restored gospel and of the Lord's infinite atonement and yet live their lives in a spirit of pessimism regarding the world's status and the likelihood the gospel will succeed in their personal lives! Then-Elder Gordon B. Hinckley counseled us: "We are the creatures of our thinking. We can talk ourselves into defeat or we can talk ourselves into victory . . . Don't partake of the spirit of our times. Look for the good and build on it. Don't be a 'pickle sucker.'"[7] We must embrace the Lord's counsel: "Let not your heart be troubled, neither let it be afraid" (John 14:27).

The tendency to look at the lives of others and to make judgment calls about what we see is a dangerous one. Certainly the Lord has cautioned us about making "unrighteous judgments" regarding the spiritual well-being of others.[8] Though we must discern good from evil so as to keep ourselves spiritually safe, it is the Lord's role to judge others. And why is it His and His alone? Because only He is capable of judging fairly. Surely all of us have had the unfortunate experience of calling into question something we have observed in another, only to find out later that we had totally misread their behavior or the circumstances. The embarrassment and shame that follow are almost indescribable. Mosiah reminded us: "Now it is better that a man should be judged of God than of man, for the judgments of God are always just, but the judgments of man are not always just" (Mosiah 29:12). So true it is. Even when we have the best of intents—the purest of motives—we cannot discern others as God sees them. There is a plethora of prophetic commentary on this issue. For example, John records the Lord's declaration: "I am he which searcheth the reins and hearts: and I will give unto every one of you according to your works" (Revelation 2:23). Isaiah states that Christ "shall not judge after the sight of his eyes, neither reprove after the hearing of his ears: But with righteousness shall he judge the poor, and reprove with equity for the meek of the earth" (Isaiah 11:3–4). In 1 Samuel 16:7 we are informed: "The Lord seeth not as man seeth; for man looketh on the outward appearance, but the Lord looketh on the heart." Many, many other similar passages could be cited.[9]

We are so prone to doubt, to doubt man's intent and ability to succeed—and to doubt God's divine plan for saving His children. Certainly most of us do not see ourselves as doubting the Lord. But, as it has been said, to despair is to turn one's back on God—to doubt Him and His promises. Thus, when we experience despair, fear, or worry, we are not exhibiting faith; we are manifesting, instead, our doubt. We should not doubt our own potential for exaltation, nor doubt the potential of others. The Lord has commanded that we "execute true judgment, and shew mercy and compassions every man to his brother" (Zechariah 7:9). President Gordon B. Hinckley counseled the Saints: "Don't be critical of people. Find their virtues—they have some—and build on those. You will be very happy if you do."[10]

In Alma 7:11–13 we learn of the Lord's atonement. Of these verses Elder Neal A. Maxwell once wrote:

> In Alma 7:12, the only place in the scriptures, to my knowledge, that it appears, there seems to have been yet another purpose of the Atonement, speaking again of the Savior and his suffering. "And he will take upon him death, that he may loose the bands of death which bind his people; and he will take upon him their infirmities, that his bowels may be filled with mercy, according to the flesh, that he may know according to the flesh how to succor his people according to their infirmities." Have you ever thought that there was no way that Jesus could know the suffering which we undergo as a result of our stupidity and sin (because he was sinless) except he bear those sins of ours in what I call the awful arithmetic of the Atonement? And according to this

> prophet, Jesus now knows, according to the flesh, how to succor us and how to help us as a result of that suffering, which knowledge could have come in no other way.[11]

Jesus didn't just suffer for our sins. Nor did He simply redeem us from the grasp of death. He suffered "pains and afflictions and temptations of every kind." He also took upon Himself all of "the pains and the sicknesses of his people" (Alma 7:11). He is intimately acquainted with us. He knows us in ways that even you and I do not know ourselves. He has suffered for every sort of pain you and I are called to endure in this mortal life—physical, spiritual, psychological, or emotional. All this He does that He can today, and on the judgment day, "succor" us (Alma 7:12). To succor is to help, aid, assist, or relieve.[12]

Because He lived the perfect, sinless life, He could not help us sinners were He left existentially unaware of the extenuating circumstances we, as fallen humans, labor under. Thus, as Alma 7:13 informs us, the Spirit enabled Christ to know exactly and experientially (through the Atonement) what it was like to be you and me—to live the lives we have, with each of the temptations we have. Jesus needed more than an intellectual understanding of what it was like to be us—what it was like to have the temptations we have, while having the background we have, and the health we have, and the family we have, and the history we have. All of these factors will be part of our judgment. Because Jesus experienced each of our lives individually, including every individual sin, pain, temptation, and so forth, Elder Maxwell has called Christ's experience the "awful arithmetic of the Atonement."[13] Christ has the composite picture. He knows all of the details. And His adding up of all things atoned for is not a negative picture of overwhelming guilt but rather a beautiful portrait of overwhelming understanding: God's understanding, and Christ's understanding, of us—of who we are, of what we need, of why we so desperately desire and merit His forgiveness.

Please know, if you're struggling, God understands why you are as you are! Because Jesus knows intimately all of these details and how they interplay in your personal life (and mine), He is able to judge us with an accuracy and love us to a depth no mortal ever could. Thanks be to the Father for His divine Plan, and to the Son, our Savior, Jesus the Christ, for His role in implementing that great plan of happiness!

Thus, when we see others struggling or seemingly going astray, we must do all we can for them. But we must never doubt or give way to despair. We must not lose hope. And we must not assume the worst. On the contrary, it is our responsibility to assume the best—and believe that all flesh is in God's hands (see D&C 101:16) and that all of our experiences are for our good (see D&C 90:24; 98:3; 105:40; 111:11)!

So much of sin that is committed is done by individuals who are not wicked or evil; they're just human. Were you to do some honest introspection you would likely have to admit that when you fall short of what you know you should be, you're racked with disappointment and regret. Most Latter-day Saints do not wish to live lives filled with sin or wickedness. But the frank reality of life is this: we are fallen men and women. We are subject to temptations, and all of us, no matter how hard we try to be good, still succumb to those enticements. In part this is because "the spirit indeed is willing, but the flesh is weak" (Matthew 26:41).

Part of our frailty stems from the fact that we labor here upon the earth under a veil of forgetfulness. The details of our premortal life in the presence of God have been blotted out. Even though the restoration of the gospel offers us a clear view of the Plan and its parameters, nonetheless, we have forgotten, much of the eternal perspective we once had. Thus, we often make choices that are contrary to our actual desires, our spiritual leanings, and our gospel understanding. We give in to the physical body because it veils the thinking of our spirit. If we could remember what we once knew—if we could think as we did when we lived in God's presence—we would surely act differently in many of the circumstances we find ourselves in. Indeed, we would be much less inclined to sin. But, alas, we do labor under a veil. And thus, often we do not see "things as they really are" (Jacob 4:13).[14] As the apostle Paul put it, "what we see now is like a dim image in a mirror" (Good News Bible, 1 Corinthians 13:12). In a sense, we really don't know what we're doing—and we certainly don't see the complete ramifications of the poor or foolish choices we make, at least not at the time we're first tempted to make them. This is not to say that the veil is a hindrance to our exaltation. To the contrary, we need it in order to learn to walk by faith and to fully exercise our divinely given agency. Nonetheless, the veil does incline us to make choices that, minus the veil, we likely would not make. Thus, the fallen man or woman we appear to be, because we're living under a veil, is not who we really are. We are God's offspring (see Acts 17:28). It was He whom we loved and worshiped in the premortal world. And it was He whom we so desperately sought to emulate—hence our desire to come to mortality that we might take the next step in our progression toward becoming as He is. The veil often obscures this fact—and causes us to forget both our premortal greatness and our eternal potential.

Commenting on Christ's request that His crucifers be forgiven ("Father, forgive them; for they know not what they do"—Luke 23:34), one commentator noted:

> Who are the "they" who "do not know what they are doing"? . . . In Luke 23:34a the "they" for whom Jesus is praying includes both the Romans and the Jews in proportion to their respective roles in Jesus's death . . . In [Luke's] understanding, no matter how much the evil was plotted, the perpetrators can always be said not to have known (i.e., appreciated God's goodness or plan) or else they would not have acted as they did. In opposing Jesus's followers to the point of stoning them, a Paul who was allied with the chief priests said: "I myself was convinced that it was necessary to do many things against the name of Jesus the Nazorean" (Acts 26:9). Yet surely Luke would judge that Paul did not know what he was doing. . . . One might sum up Luke's attitude thus: If there were those who did not know because they had not been told, there were also those who did not know because, although they had been told, they did not grasp.[15]

In other words, just as Jesus could say, "Forgive them, for they know not what they do," it can be said of all who sin, "They know not what they do." For, which of us, having an eternal perspective restored to us, would continue to do things which we know to be contrary to God's will?

When we look upon those steeped in sin or those tempted to stray from the path, we must, with Christ, petition the Father to forgive them. We must assume the best of them and part of that "best" is recognizing that most people commit sin because "they know not what they do." It is the Lord's place to judge their hearts and their choices. It is our place to unconditionally love them as He loves them.

Now much has been made of the role of righteous parents and families in the return of the "prodigal" son or daughter. As with everything else we've said, we must acknowledge that the Lord is the only one who can judge. Nonetheless, we are on safe ground if we do no more than cite that which the Brethren have given on this subject.

Mosiah recorded the words of an angel spoken to the wayward Alma the Younger regarding the influence his righteous father (Alma the Elder) had had upon his son's salvation.

> And again, the angel said: Behold, the Lord hath heard the prayers of his people, and also the prayers of his servant, Alma, who is thy father; for he has prayed with much faith concerning thee that thou mightest be brought to the knowledge of the truth; therefore, for this purpose have I come to

> convince thee of the power and authority of God, that the prayers of his servants might be answered according to their faith. (Mosiah 27:14)

It is unclear exactly when and why the Lord chooses to answer such prayers and intervene. All that we're told is this: Alma and other righteous souls prayed on behalf of Alma the Younger; God heard those prayers; and in response to what He heard, the Father sent an angel to intervene. In the end the "rules of engagement" matter little. All that matters is that faith was exhibited, God acknowledged it, and via His intervention a life was changed for the better. The Prophet Joseph once remarked: "When a seal is put upon the father and mother, it secures their posterity, so that they cannot be lost, but will be saved by virtue of the covenant of their father and mother."[16] Howard Cory, the personal secretary of the Prophet Joseph, recorded the following words as he heard them fall from the lips of President Smith: "A measure of this sealing is to confirm upon their head in common with Elijah the doctrine of election or the covenant with Abraham—which when a Father & mother of a family have entered into[,] their children who have not transgressed are secured by the seal wherewith the Parents have been sealed."[17]

In the September 2002 *Ensign,* an article appeared under the title "Hope for Parents of Wayward Children." In that article four quotes were offered in support of the idea that the faithfulness of parents can indeed influence the ultimate salvation of their children. Two of those remarks were from presidents of the

Church, two from members of the Quorum of the Twelve Apostles.

The first of these assurances was from Elder Orson F. Whitney of the Twelve. Elder Whitney said in the April 1929 general conference:

> The Prophet Joseph Smith declared—and he never taught more comforting doctrine—that the eternal sealings of faithful parents and the divine promises made to them for valiant service in the Cause of Truth, would save not only themselves, but likewise their posterity. Though some of the sheep may wander, the eye of the Shepherd is upon them, and sooner or later they will feel the tentacles of Divine Providence reaching out after them and drawing them back to the fold. Either in this life or the life to come, they will return. They will have to pay their debt to justice; they will suffer for their sins; and may tread a thorny path; but if it leads them at last, like the penitent Prodigal, to a loving and forgiving father's heart and home, the painful experience will not have been in vain. Pray for your careless and disobedient children; hold on to them with your faith. Hope on, trust on, till you see the salvation of God.[18]

The second quotation comes from President Brigham Young. He is quoted as having taught something similar to Elder Whitney, but with a slight clarification. Said President Young:

> Let the father and mother, who are members of this Church and kingdom, take a righteous course, and strive

> with all their might never to do a wrong, but to do good all their lives; if they have one child or one hundred children, if they conduct themselves towards them as they should, binding them to the Lord by their faith and prayers, I care not where those children go, they are bound up to their parents by an everlasting tie, and no power of earth or hell can separate them from their parents in eternity; they will return again to the fountain from whence they sprang.[19]

Quotation number three comes from President Lorenzo Snow, from a discourse he delivered in the October 1893 general conference of the Church. He stated:

> If you succeed in passing through these trials and afflictions and receive a resurrection, you will, by the power of the Priesthood, work and labor, as the Son of God has, until you get all your sons and daughters in the path of exaltation and glory. This is just as sure as that the sun rose this morning over yonder mountains. Therefore, mourn not because all your sons and daughters do not follow in the path that you have marked out to them, or give heed to your counsels. Inasmuch as we succeed in securing eternal glory, and stand as saviors, and as kings and priests to our God, we will save our posterity.[20]

The final quotation in that article is from President Boyd K. Packer, Acting President of the Quorum of the Twelve Apostles. President Packer stated:

> The measure of our success as parents . . . will not rest solely on how our children turn out. That judgment would be just only if we could raise our families in a perfectly moral environment, and that now is not possible. It is not uncommon for responsible parents to lose one of their children, for a time, to influences over which they have no control. They agonize over rebellious sons or daughters. They are puzzled over why they are so helpless when they have tried so hard to do what they should. It is my conviction that those wicked influences one day will be overruled . . . We cannot overemphasize the value of temple marriage, the binding ties of the sealing ordinance, and the standards of worthiness required of them. When parents keep the covenants they have made at the altar of the temple, their children will be forever bound to them.[21]

Many have queried how the declarations made in this Church-approved article[22] will come to pass without robbing the wayward children referred to of their divinely given agency. The article does not say. We are left to ourselves, only with the conviction that God cannot lie—and His divinely appointed servants cannot lead us astray.[23] In response to this article, Joseph Fielding McConkie wrote: "Of this I think there can be no question—Each of these men are teaching that the man and woman united together by the authority of the temple have a power and capacity to save their children—including the wayward—that reaches far beyond that which we have imagined. This, however, does not suggest any shortcuts to the glories of eternity."[24] Elsewhere Brother McConkie reasoned:

Let us ask, Can bitterness and opposition to the kingdom of God bequeath a negative inheritance to a person's children? In the dedicatory prayer of the Kirtland Temple, the Prophet asked the Lord to make bare his arm in protecting his people from enemies who had done much to afflict them. He prayed, "May thine anger be kindled, and thine indignation fall upon them, that they may be wasted away, both root and branch, from under heaven" (D&C 109:52). In response to that plea, we read in a subsequent revelation, "not many years hence, . . . they [the persecutors] and their posterity shall be swept from under heaven, saith God, that not one of them is left to stand by the wall." Of those who swore falsely against the Lord's anointed the revelation stated: "They shall not have right to the priesthood, nor their posterity after them from generation to generation" (D&C 121:15, 21). Surely, if the blood of those who fought against the Lord is to be remembered from generation to generation, so the posterity of the faithful will be remembered in the blessings of the Lord. . . . Consider the language used to describe the return of the keys, or the authority, by which the eternal family unit is formed: "Elias appeared, and committed the dispensation of the gospel of Abraham, saying that in us and our seed all generations after us should be blessed" (D&C 110:12). Surely the promise of blessings to future generations spoken of here would embrace their own posterity. Indeed, it was through their posterity that future generations were to be blessed.[25]

Perhaps President Joseph F. Smith's vision of the redemption of the dead offers a subtle bit of clarification. That revelation reads in part: "The dead who repent will be redeemed, through obedience to the ordinances of the house of God, And *after they have paid the penalty* of their transgressions, and are washed clean, shall receive a reward according to their works, for they are heirs of salvation" (D&C 138:58–59; emphasis added). In some way, unexplained by the presiding Brethren, there is a power resident in the sealing of a faithful husband and wife. That power extends to their children, and it binds families forever.[26] Such a knowledge brings with it a spirit of optimism and implies, once again, "odds are, you're going to be exalted!" I do not understand how it is so. I do not know what will be required of those who, to mortal eyes, appear to have strayed. As the Lord said through His prophet Isaiah, "For my thoughts are not your thoughts, neither are your ways my ways, saith the Lord. For as the heavens are higher than the earth, so are my ways higher than your ways, and my thoughts than your thoughts" (Isaiah 55:8–9). The Lord's ways and thoughts are above and beyond mine. They are to me, a finite human being, in many ways incomprehensible. In a nutshell, I don't need to understand how God will save the seemingly wayward children of faithful, sealed parents. All I need know is that God knows what He is doing. I simply have to have faith in the declarations and promises of the Lord's anointed, such as this comment from a modern-day apostle:

> You parents of the wilful and the wayward! Don't give them up. Don't cast them off. They are not utterly lost. The

> Shepherd will find his sheep. They were his before they were yours—long before he entrusted them to your care; and you cannot begin to love them as he loves them. They have but strayed in ignorance from the Path of Right, and God is merciful to ignorance.[27]

Similarly, in the same discussion in which the Prophet Joseph stated: "When a seal is put upon the father and mother, it secures their posterity, so that they cannot be lost, but will be saved by virtue of the covenant of their father and mother,"[28] he added this warning: "It is the constitutional disposition of mankind to set up stakes and set bounds to the works and ways of the Almighty . . . I say to all those who are disposed to set up stakes for the Almighty, [if you do so,] You will come short of the glory of God. To become a joint heir of the heirship of the Son, one must put away all his false traditions."[29] We must not doubt when we see those around us struggle. And we must never cease to call upon God on their behalf. But we must also ever keep in mind that, if *you* worry about and pray for *your* children, God the Father is a thousand times more attentive to the needs and spiritual well-being of *His* children than is even the best of mortal parents. And just as you and I would do anything within our power to save our sons and daughters, the all powerful God will do the same. It seems that none of us is authorized to say more than that.

CHAPTER SEVEN

CONCLUSION

Having come full circle, some will feel relief at the good news that there is a loving Father in Heaven who has designed a plan that will exalt *all* who truly desire to be exalted. Others, no doubt, will fight against the truths expressed herein, preferring instead (as one author put it) to "perish rather than accept the grace of God because it seems to them too easy."[1] Can it be so? Can it really be as easy as described? And if so, can it be that some will nonetheless reject the good news, preferring instead a more difficult way?

Thankfully exaltation *is* obtainable in the simple manner described. And tragically, some *do* desire a more difficult way, rather than to simply reach out to embrace the Lord and His Plan![2] Elder George Teasdale of the Quorum of the Twelve Apostles once noted: "Straight is the way and narrow is the path that leadeth to the exaltations, and few there be that find it. Why? Because they do not want it."[3] Similarly, President Brigham Young taught: "Can you save all? Yes, you can save all that will be [or desire to be] saved. If people are not saved, it is because they are not disposed to be saved."[4] President Young went on to say: "God will save all who are determined to be saved."[5] Now it may sound silly to say that some do not want exaltation. Yet, when we reject the declarations of God and His prophets regarding the easiness of the way, what else can we conclude but that we somehow do not want what God freely offers? Consider the following scriptural stories and how they illustrate the attitude we have been speaking of.

In the Old Testament we read of Naaman the leper, who came to the prophet Elisha because Naaman desired to be healed. However, when Elisha's council was for Naaman to simply wash seven times in the Jordan River it was too much—or, better put, too little—to ask! Naaman went away enraged (see 2 Kings 5:10–12), disdaining to do what the prophet had advised him. He wanted something more complex, more difficult. He couldn't believe that the miracle of healing could come in such a simple way, just as many of us cannot believe that the miracle of spiritual healing can come in the very simple way described in scriptures, and in this book.

There is also the well-known Old Testament story of the children of Israel being attacked by "fiery serpents" (Numbers 21:6; see vv. 8–9). In response to that attack, and the deaths that followed, Moses was commanded to lift up a brass serpent upon a pole and to instruct those bitten by the poisonous snakes to look upon the brass serpent in faith. "And as many as should look upon that serpent should live, even so as many as should look upon the Son of

God with faith, having a contrite spirit, might live, even unto that life which is eternal" (Helaman 8:15). So easy an act; so few willing to comply. Reflecting on this lack of faith, Alma records: "But few understood the meaning of those things, and this because of the hardness of their hearts. But there were many who were so hardened that they would not look, therefore they perished. Now the reason they would not look is because they did not believe that it would heal them" (Alma 33:20). And why did they not believe? Again, apparently they could not believe that God would give relief so readily. Likewise, some of us find it hard to believe God would give relief from sin and suffering so readily—but He does! I testify that He does!

For reasons unknown to me, some, regardless of the logic and prophetic teachings on the subject, will ever feel that God simply could not be as kind as He is described in the pages of this small book. And yet He is. He *is* that kind, and His Plan is that simple! Elder Neal A. Maxwell once noted: "The gospel of Jesus Christ is simple. Just because something is simple does not mean it is untrue. Jacob warned about the danger of preferring complexity, of 'looking beyond the mark,' and of seeking a tangled theology that people 'cannot understand.' (Jacob 4:14.)"[6]

Yes, we must strive to keep the commandments—for there is not "cheap grace." But the frank reality is that none of us will succeed in doing so to the standard required, or even to the degree we are capable. That's where Christ's atonement must come in. As the Prophet Joseph Smith taught: "God does not look on sin with allowance, but when men have sinned, there must be allowance made for them."[7] The Atonement is that "allowance" that will address our failings. We must but desire to be good—to do our best (and our best will differ from day to day)! But with Jacob we declare, "O the wisdom of God, his mercy and grace!" (2 Nephi 9:8). The Savior has provided the means for our redemption; not because He had to, but because He loves us. He loves us with the purest and deepest of love; a degree of love incomprehensible to you and me. "O how great the goodness of our God, who prepareth a way for our escape from the grasp of this awful monster; yea, that monster, death and hell, which I call the death of the body, and also the death of the spirit" (2 Nephi 9:10). All that He does—*all that He does*—is for "the everlasting welfare of your souls" (2 Nephi 2:30). As Yale University chaplain William Sloane Coffin once stated: "God has more grace than you and I have sins."[8] Who of us is so numb to the Spirit of God that we can not feel it testifying to the truthfulness of those words? Oh, that we could muster the faith to firmly trust in the declaration: "The Lord will never give up his mercy" (Ecclesiasticus 47:22).

Of the Father's immensely merciful character, the Prophet Joseph Smith said: "Our heavenly Father is more liberal in His views, and boundless in His mercies and blessings, than we are ready to believe or receive."[9] President J. Reuben Clark Jr., of the First Presidency, stated:

> I believe that his juridical concept of his dealings with his children could be expressed in this way: I believe that in his justice and mercy he will give us the maximum reward for

> our acts, give us all that he can give, and in the reverse, I believe that he will impose upon us the minimum penalty which it is possible for him to impose.[10]

Similarly, Elder Orson F. Whitney, of the Twelve, taught: "Our Heavenly Father is far more merciful, infinitely more charitable, than even the best of his servants, and the Everlasting Gospel is mightier in power to save than our narrow finite minds can comprehend."[11] And more recently, Elder Jeffrey R. Holland stated: "The Father of us all . . . is divinely anxious to bless us this very moment. Mercy is his mission, and love is his only labor."[12] Around the time he was called to serve as an Apostle, Elder Bruce R. McConkie penned these words—the lyrics to the hymn "I Believe in Christ":

> *I believe in Christ; he stands supreme!*
> *From him I'll gain my fondest dream;*
> *And while I strive through grief and pain,*
> *His voice is heard: "Ye shall obtain."*[13]

Elder McConkie clearly saw the Father in optimistic terms. "Ye shall obtain!" What sweet words to hear from the lips of Him who created all things! I firmly believe that nothing would please the Father more than to extend to us "our fondest dream." Indeed, it is His "fondest dream" to have as many of His children return home to Him as desire so to do. And it is His intent to make that happen. Thus, the Prophet Joseph Smith taught that "the kindness of our Heavenly Father [calls] for our heartfelt gratitude."[14] And so it does!

In the hymn "I Know That My Redeemer Lives," we learn of Jesus' desire to secure our salvation. In the first three verses of that sacred song, we are reminded: "He lives to bless me with his love. / He lives to plead for me above."[15] "He lives all blessings to impart."[16] "He lives my mansion to prepare. / He lives to bring me safely there."[17] Echoing the words of this hymn are the words of the Lord Himself:

> Listen to him who is the advocate with the Father, who is pleading your cause before him—Saying: Father, behold the sufferings and death of him who did no sin, in whom thou wast well pleased; behold the blood of thy Son which was shed, the blood of him whom thou gavest that thyself might be glorified; Wherefore, Father, spare these my brethren that believe on my name, that they may come unto me and have everlasting life. (D&C 45:3–5)

Can there be any doubt that Christ desires our complete and total forgiveness and our redemption? Can there be any doubt as to how the Father will respond to His Only Begotten's plea? Given the price Christ so selflessly paid in Gethsemane and on Golgotha's cross, could a just God—and loving Father—do other that accept Christ's request on our behalf? The Spirit's answer is a resounding "No!"

Our part in our salvation is important—as are our sincere efforts to accomplish what God has asked of us. But we must keep in mind His mercy, and keep in context His commands. God knows we're going to fall short. His expectation of us is not perfection but an attitude of willingness to endure, sorrow for sin, and a determination to move ourselves bit by bit toward Him in our nature, thoughts, desires, and actions. Hugh Nibley frequently referred to the "Doctrine of the Two Ways,"[18] which is this: You're either drawing closer to God or closer to the devil. You're either moving toward exaltation or toward damnation. The issue is not the rate at which you're traveling. What matters is that you're on the road, and you're heading in the right direction. Not everyone can move at the spiritual speed of a Paul, or a Joseph Smith, or a Gordon B. Hinckley. But, thankfully, none of us will be judged in comparison to those Brethren. We will only be judged in comparison to ourselves—our progress, our efforts to stay headed in the right direction, our sincere attempts to always associate with the sanctifying influence of the Holy Ghost. What others do, or do not do, has no bearing on us. All we need ask ourselves is this: "Am I on the path? Am I facing the right direction? Am I moving forward?" Little more is asked of us by God.

God does not seek to condemn us based upon some "loophole" in the law. To the contrary, He seeks to save us by applying any and every "loophole" He can. He will not condemn us for our petty imperfections, only for our willful rebellion.[19] President J. Reuben Clark Jr., of the First Presidency, stated:

> I believe that our Heavenly Father wants to save every one of his children. I do not think he intends to shut any of

> us off because of some slight transgression, some slight failure to observe some rule or regulation. There are the great elementals that we must observe, but he is not going to be captious[20] about the lesser things.[21]

Likewise, Joseph Smith said that we should be merciful to others—and overlook their small faults and failings—just as God overlooks ours. Joseph rhetorically asked: "Suppose that Jesus Christ and holy angels should object to us on frivolous things, what would become of us?" Then he added, we must be like God and Christ. "We must be merciful to one another, and overlook small things . . . To the iniquitous show yourselves merciful."[22] Major sins unaddressed will bring significant consequences. However, petty failings caused by our human side will receive of God's forgiveness, mercy, and grace, if we seek it.[23]

When Jesus was teaching Nicodemus, He reminded the inquiring Pharisee that His divine mission was not to bring damnation, but rather to bring life. Jesus said: "For *God sent not his Son into the world to condemn the world;* but that the world through him might be saved" (John 3:17; emphasis added). Not only is "happiness . . . the object and design of our existence,"[24] but it is the "work" and the "glory" of the Father, Son, and Holy Spirit—to "bring to pass the immortality and eternal life of man" (Moses 1:39). And such will be the outcome of the great plan of happiness for all who wish it so to be! In this spirit, the Prophet Joseph Smith extended this comforting invitation: "Therefore, dearly beloved brethren, let us cheerfully do all things that lie in our power; and then may we stand still, with the utmost assurance, to see the salvation of God, and for his arm to be revealed" (D&C 123:17). And Elder Bruce R. McConkie has also assured us: "Though you haven't fully overcome the world and you haven't done all you hoped you might do—you're still going to be saved."[25]

A number of years ago I heard Elder Jeffrey R. Holland of the Quorum of the Twelve say to a group of Stanford University students, "God is not like an umpire waiting to call you 'out' at home plate."[26] He is more like the third base coach who watches out for you and who urges you safely on to home. When you're hoping to score a home run, you have to trust that coach who urges you on. You can't pause to look over your shoulder, and you can't call into question his judgment. You know he wants you to score—perhaps just as badly as you want to. So you work together to make it happen. So it is with Father in Heaven. He urges us on. He lets us know how very close we are. He wants us to succeed—to safely make it home—just as badly as we do. And yet, He can see better than we do, and we must trust His judgment and follow His direction.

Elder Holland shared the following experience, which highlights the need, in those hours of doubt, to accept the assurances that have been offered in this book. Elder Holland said:

> Katie Lewis is my neighbor. Her father, Randy, is my bishop; her mother, Melanie, is a saint. And her older brother, Jimmie, is battling leukemia. Sister Lewis recently recounted for me the unspeakable fear and grief that came to

their family when Jimmie's illness was diagnosed. She spoke of the tears and the waves of sorrow that any mother would experience with a prognosis as grim as Jimmie's was. But like the faithful Latter-day Saints they are, the Lewises turned to God with urgency and with faith and with hope. They fasted and prayed, prayed and fasted. And they went again and again to the temple. One day Sister Lewis came home from a temple session weary and worried, feeling the impact of so many days—and nights—of fear being held at bay only by *monumental* faith. As she entered her home, four-year-old Katie ran up to her with love in her eyes and a crumpled sheaf of papers in her hand. Holding the papers out to her mother, she said enthusiastically, "Mommy, do you know what these are?" Sister Lewis said frankly her first impulse was to deflect Katie's zeal and say she didn't feel like playing just then. But she thought of her children—all her children—and the possible regret of missed opportunities and little lives that pass too swiftly. So she smiled through her sorrow and said, "No, Katie. I don't know what they are. Please tell me." "They are the scriptures," Katie beamed back, "and do you know what they say?" Sister Lewis stopped smiling, gazed deeply at this little child, knelt down to her level, and said, "Tell me, Katie. What do the scriptures say?" "They say, '*Trust Jesus.*'" And then she was gone. Sister Lewis said that as she stood back up, holding a fistful of her four-year-old's scribbling, she felt near-tangible arms of peace encircle her weary soul and a divine stillness calm her troubled heart. Katie Lewis, "angel and minister of grace,"

> I'm with you. In a world of some discouragement, sorrow, and overmuch sin, in times when fear and despair seem to prevail, when humanity is feverish with no worldly physicians in sight, I too say, "Trust Jesus." Let him still the tempest and ride upon the storm. Believe that he can lift mankind from its bed of affliction, in time and in eternity. *Oh, dearly, dearly has he loved! And we must love him too, And trust in his redeeming blood, And try his works to do.*[27]

"Trust Jesus!" That is what we must do. And trust the Father, too! You and I know Their nature. We know Their character. We're intimately acquainted with Their constant and unflinching goodness, mercy, love, concern, and commitment to each of us. We know They want us to succeed. We must not forget this. We must trust Them, and trust in the Plan They have designed specifically to exalt each of us. As the Lord, Himself, stated:

> For I came down from heaven, not to do mine own will, but the will of him that sent me. And this is the Father's will which hath sent me, that of *all* which he hath given me I should lose *nothing,* but should raise it up again at the last day. And this is the will of him that sent me, that *every one* which seeth the Son, and believeth on him, may have everlasting life: and I will raise him up at the last day. (John 6:38–40; emphasis added)

Clearly Jesus and the Father intended the salvation and exaltation of all who would believe. They desired the damnation and loss of none. And Jesus was sent to bring to pass the Father's desire and will. When we heard the Plan and its parameters and requirements presented in the premortal world, we "trusted Jesus" and we "trusted the Father." We knew they would not place us in a dangerous scenario. Let us not forget that we shouted for joy when the Father revealed to us this plan. We sang "the song of redeeming love" when He presented it. With Alma, "I would ask, can ye feel so now?" (Alma 5:26). Oh, how we must!

The message of the scriptures is a positive and assuring one. The message of the restored gospel is likewise a positive and an assuring one. The message of the Holy Spirit is a positive and an assuring one. Indeed, President Heber C. Kimball once said: "I am perfectly satisfied that my Father and my God is a cheerful, pleasant, lively, and good-natured Being. Why? Because I am cheerful, pleasant, lively, and good-natured when I have His Spirit."[28] If our lives are saturated in God's Holy Spirit we cannot feel pessimistic about our salvation. We should only feel joy and anticipation for what is shortly to be ours. As we previously noted, then-Elder Gordon B. Hinckley counseled us, "Don't be a pickle sucker!"[29] There is no place for pessimism in this Church, and there is no place for it on the road to exaltation! The message of the restored gospel is one of "good news"—and in addition to all of the "good news" we are wont to preach, there is the infrequently spoken fact, "Odds are, you're going to be exalted!"

Of this I testify.

Notes

Introduction

1. Millet, *Within Reach,* 3.
2. Millet, *Alive in Christ,* 172–73.
3. Nelson, "Perfection Pending," *Ensign,* Nov. 1995, 86.
4. Young, *Discourses,* 64.
5. Packer, "Great Plan of Happiness."

Chapter One: The Role of Commandments

1. We are told in 2 Nephi 2:5 that "by the law [or commandments] no flesh is justified." And why are we not justified by the commandments? Because we do not *fully* keep them. The law could only save us if we, like Christ, were fully obedient to it. But since you and I fall short of perfection, we cannot save ourselves though obedience.

2. Kelly, *Early Christian Doctrines,* 352, 356, 374.

3. The following scriptures are often quoted—or, perhaps better put, misquoted—to show that works have *no* role in the receipt of salvation. However, each of these passages actually condemns the "works" of the law of Moses and not the performance of "good works" in the image and pattern of Christ with the intent of both worshiping God and conforming oneself to His image and nature. Since the law of Moses had been fulfilled in Christ, its works, rituals, and obligations had no salvific effect for Jews or Christians. Because of

Christ's atonement, reliance upon the works of that former system could not bring salvation. In each of the passages that follow, Paul is condemning the fulfilled "law" and not the "good works" that of necessity follow any true Christian's conversion to Christ. Romans 3:1, 20, 27–31 tell us that the deeds of the law of Moses cannot justify us in God's sight. "No one will attain the status of uprightness before God's tribunal by performing deeds mandated by the Mosaic law. . . . These are not simply 'good deeds,' but those performed in obedience to the law and regarded by Jews as the means of preserving their covenantal status before God" (Fitzmyer, *Romans,* 337). Romans 11:3–6 indicates that being given the gospel is the result of God's grace and not of works. One commentator wrote: "What Paul objects to is 'works' understood as a qualification for God's favor simply because it is they which qualify for membership of the covenant people and which sustain that identity as God's elect. It is this *reduction* of God's election to matters of ethnic and ritual identity which Paul sees as the fatal misunderstanding and abandonment of God's grace" (Dunn, *Romans 9–16,* 647; emphasis in original; see also Bruce, *Romans,* 201). Galatians 2:16 states that the "works of the law" of Moses simply have no power to justify us, but our faith in Christ can. "All Jewish Christians . . . had initially agreed that it was utterly impossible to commend themselves to God by law-keeping. . . . [T]he present insistence of the Judaizers on the keeping of the law [of Moses] is utterly at variance with their own basic belief" (Cole, *Galatians,* 120). Ephesians 2:8–10, 14–16 indicates that "a true believer will never boast that his coming to faith, his solid stance in faith, and his (ethical) demonstration of faith are of his own doing" (Barth, *Ephesians 1–3,* 225). Another wrote: "What the apostle wants to say is that the whole initiative and every aspect of the making available of this salvation is God's. . . .

"Then, secondly, we are taken back to the terminology of Romans and Galatians—*not because of works*—and to what was a vital question for the Jews of Paul's day because of their exaltation of the law [of Moses]" (Foulkes, *Ephesians,* 84; emphasis in original). Of course, none of these four passages is suggesting that doing "good works," or striving to keep the commandments, is wrong. The primary concern in each of the aforementioned selections is the law of Moses and Israel's tendency to rely upon it instead of Christ. The Holy Bible is quite clear on the idea that "good works" are a necessary manifestation of true faith in Christ and the attainment of salvation (see, for example,

Philippians 2:12—"Work out your own salvation"; 2 Timothy 4:14—"The Lord reward . . . according to his works"; James 2:14, 17–24, 26—"Faith without works is dead"; 1 Peter 1:16–17—The Father judges us according to our works; Revelation 2:23, 26—God gives "according to [our] works"; Revelation 14:13—"Their works do follow them [the dead]"; Revelation 20:12–13—All of us will be judged "according to [our] works"; Revelation 22:12—God rewards every man according to his works). Other passages imply that one must have more than simple belief in order to be "saved," as true faith presupposes action on the part of the believer (see, for example, Matthew 5:48—"Be ye therefore perfect"; Matthew 7:19–23—Only those who do God's will go to heaven; Matthew 24:13—"Endure unto the end . . . [and] be saved"; Mark 13:13—"Endure unto the end . . . [and] be saved"; Mark 16:16–18—"Signs shall follow them that believe"; John 14:15—"If ye love me, keep my commandments"; 1 John 3:8—"He that committeth sin is of the devil").

4. In 2 Nephi 4:34 we read: "O Lord, I have trusted in thee, and I will trust in thee forever. I will not put my trust in the arm of flesh; for I know that cursed is he that putteth his trust in the arm of flesh. Yea, cursed is he that putteth his trust in man or maketh flesh his arm." We must try as hard as we can to do what is right. But we must never believe that it will be our works and righteousness that will save us. Such inclinations to lean on the "arm of flesh" will always prove disastrous, as none of us will ever succeed. I hesitate to say we don't have what it takes, because we really do—what it takes is a Savior, and we have that in Christ. But we do not have within us the ability to live as He lived, and for that reason alone reliance upon, or trust in, the "arm of flesh" will always prove unsuccessful.

5. Robinson, *Believing Christ,* 91–90. In explaining this passage, Robinson writes: "In my opinion some of the blame for our misapplication of gospel superlatives and other similarly obsessive reasoning comes from a misunderstanding of 2 Nephi 25:23: 'For we labor diligently to write, to persuade our children, and also our brethren, to believe in Christ, and to be reconciled to God; for we know that it is by grace that we are saved, *after* all we can do.' (Italics added.)

"At first glance at this scripture, we might think that grace is offered to us only chronologically after we have completed doing all we can do, but this is demonstrably false, for we have already received many manifestations of God's grace before we even come to this point. By his grace, we live and breathe. . . .

" . . . I understand the preposition 'after' in 2 Nephi 25:23 to be a preposition of separation rather than a preposition of time. It denotes logical separateness rather than temporal sequence. We are saved by grace 'apart from all we can do,' or 'all we can do notwithstanding,' or even 'regardless of all we can do.' Another acceptable paraphrase of the sense of the verse might read, 'We are still saved by grace, after all is said and done.'

"In addition, even the phrase 'all we can do' is susceptible to a sinister interpretation as meaning every single good deed we could conceivably have ever done. This is nonsense. If grace could operate only in such cases, no one could ever be saved, not even the best among us. It is precisely because we *don't* always do everything we could have done that we need a savior in the first place, so obviously we can't make doing everything we could have done a condition for receiving grace and being saved! I believe the emphasis in 2 Nephi 25:23 is meant to fall on the word *we* ('all *we* can do,' as opposed to all *he* can do). Moreover, 'all we can do' here should probably be understood in the sense of 'everything we can do,' or even 'whatever we can do.'

"Thus, the correct sense of 2 Nephi 25:23 would be that we are ultimately saved by grace apart from whatever we manage to do. Grace is not merely a decorative touch or a finishing bit of trim to top off our own efforts—it is God's participation in the process of our salvation from its beginning to its end. Though I must be intimately involved in the process of my salvation, in the long run the success of that venture is utterly dependent upon the grace of Christ" (90–92).

6. As Elder Wilford Woodruff put it, "This Gospel is everlasting in its nature and unchangeable in its character" (*Journal of Discourses,* 8:265).

7. The Prophet Joseph Smith said: "It was the design of the councils of heaven before the world was, that the principles and laws of the priesthood should be predicated upon the gathering of the people in every age of the world. . . . Ordinances instituted in the heavens before the foundation of the world, in the priesthood, for the salvation of men, are not to be altered or changed. All must be saved on the same principles" (*Teachings,* 308). See also the poetic version of Doctrine and Covenants 76, often referred to as "A Vision," in *Times and Seasons* 4 (1 Feb. 1843): 82–83.

8. Smith, *Teachings,* 345–46; emphasis in original. See also *History of the Church,* 6:306; *Joseph Smith,* 221.

9. Talmage, in Conference Report, Apr. 1915, 123.

10. Young, in *Journal of Discourses,* 11:249. On another occasion President Young stated: "The heavenly hosts are beings . . . *having passed through the same ordeals we are now passing through*" (ibid., 8:81; emphasis added). He also explained: "Angels are those beings who have been on an earth like this, and *have passed through the same ordeals that we are now passing through. . . .* All the difference between men and angels is, men are passing through the day of trial that angels have already passed through" (ibid., 9:102; emphasis added).

11. Cannon, in *Journal of Discourses,* 25:26; emphasis added.

12. McConkie, *New Witness,* 64; emphasis added.

13. President Joseph F. Smith taught: "We are precisely in the same condition and under the same circumstances that God our heavenly Father was when he was passing through this, or a similar ordeal" (*Gospel Doctrine,* 64). Elder Wilford Woodruff stated that God the Father "had His endowments long ago; it is thousands and millions of years since He received His [temple] blessings" (*Journal of Discourses,* 4:192). Latter-day Saint scholars have also highlighted the truth that God the Father became what He is by obedience to eternal laws and ordinances of the everlasting gospel. Joseph Fielding McConkie wrote: "God was once a man obtaining his exalted status *by obedience to the laws* of his own eternal Father" (*Answers,* 168; emphasis added). Kent P. Jackson penned this: "God was once a man *in a probationary status* similar to our own" (*Apostasy to Restoration,* 246; emphasis added).

14. Smith, *Teachings,* 345.

15. Talmage, *Jesus the Christ,* 540.

16. Ogden and Skinner, *Four Gospels,* 536; emphasis in original.

17. In Alma 42:25 we read: "What, do ye suppose that mercy can rob justice? I say unto you, Nay; not one whit. If so, God would cease to be God." I have often heard Latter-day Saints quote Alma 42 as if to prove that God cannot be merciful to us sinful human beings. Of this verse, President Joseph Fielding Smith once wrote: "The mercy of the Lord is wonderful. It does not rob justice, for they work in perfect harmony" (*Way to Perfection,* 200). Members of the Church must remember that Christ's atonement satisfies the demands of justice so that mercy *cannot* rob it. Thus, even if someone is a flawed

human being his or her entire life, if he or she is repentant at heart, Christ's atonement can then step in and satisfy the demands of justice, allowing mercy to cover the regretful sinner's shortcomings. The only way in which mercy would rob justice is if Christ's atonement covered the sins of those who felt no remorse for the wrongs they had knowingly done. Thus, mercy *never* robs justice in the lives of those who seek to be better humans. That "mercy cannot rob justice" is the very reason why the Father commissioned Christ's atonement from the "foundations of the world." Elder B. H. Roberts wrote: "In the atonement there is a nice balancing of the relative claims of justice and mercy. The law given to man having been transgressed, justice demanded the payment of the penalty, which was death. And as Adam had no power to liberate himself from the captivity thereof, his sleep in the grave must have been eternal; so also with all his posterity to whom his mortality was bequeathed as an evil legacy, had not Mercy put in her claims and prevented Justice from being cruel. The Son of God having it given to him to have life in himself, and being capable of making an infinite atonement, he stood forth as the great friend of man and offered himself as a sacrifice to satisfy the claims of Justice. That offering was accepted by the great Law Giver, and upon the demands of Justice being satisfied,—the law having no further claim upon him,—the captive is set free from the dominion of death. Mercy is not permitted to rob Justice, but she claims her own. Justice is not permitted to be cruel, but he retains his dignity—his demands are satisfied. As the late President Taylor very beautifully says: 'Is justice dishonored? No; it is satisfied; the debt is paid. Is righteousness departed from? No; there is a righteous act. All requirements are met. Is judgment violated? No; its demands are fulfilled. Is Mercy triumphant? No; she simply claims her own. Justice, judgment, mercy and truth all harmonize as the attributes of Deity. Justice and truth have met together, righteousness and peace have kissed each other, justice and judgment triumph as well as mercy and peace; all the attributes of Deity harmonize in this great, grand, momentous, just, equitable, merciful and meritorious act'" (*Outlines of Ecclesiastical History,* 95–96).

18. Maxwell, *Evening with a General Authority,* 2 Feb. 2001. See also Maxwell, *Promise of Discipleship,* 80–81.

19. Grant, in Stuy, *Collected Discourses,* 4:355–56.

20. Evans, in Conference Report, Apr. 1955, 21.

21. Hafen and Hafen, *Belonging Heart,* 287.

22. Charles H. Gabriel, "I Stand All Amazed," *Hymns,* no. 193. The entirety of verses 1 and 2 reads as follows:

> *I stand all amazed at the love Jesus offers me,*
> *Confused at the grace that so fully he proffers me.*
> *I tremble to know that for me he was crucified,*
> *That for me, a sinner, he suffered, he bled and died.*
>
> *I marvel that he would descend from his throne divine*
> *To rescue a soul so rebellious and proud as mine,*
> *That he should extend his great love unto such as I,*
> *Sufficient to own, to redeem, and to justify.*

Chapter Two: A Plan That Will Maximize Returns

1. Packer, "Great Plan of Happiness."

2. It is common for Latter-day Saints to make a distinction between "salvation" and "exaltation." And while it is true that there is a difference between being resurrected (or "saved") and inheriting the highest degree of the celestial kingdom (or "exaltation"), in most cases when the prophets speak of "salvation," they are referring to "exaltation" or eternal life—and not simply resurrection. President Marion G. Romney taught: "*Saved* . . . means resurrected and returned as a sanctified, celestialized, immortal soul to the presence and society of God, there to pursue an endless course of eternal progress" ("How Men Are Saved," *Ensign,* Nov. 1974, 38). Likewise, Robert L. Millet wrote: "With but few exceptions, however, when the prophets speak of salvation they are referring to the highest of eternal rewards hereafter. . . . In the ultimate meaning, to be saved is to qualify for exaltation in the celestial kingdom" (*Within Reach,* 75).

3. Of course, exaltation is dwelling for eternity in the highest degree of the celestial kingdom. Anyone in any other degree of the celestial kingdom, or in any other kingdom, is, by definition, damned (see Richard Neitzel Holzapfel, "Damnation," in Ludlow et al., *Encyclopedia of Mormonism,* 1:353; Margaret McConkie Pope, "Exaltation," in ibid., 2:479; N. Gaylon Hopkins, "Joint-Heirs with Christ," in ibid., 2:583; Dillon K. Inouye, "Celibacy," in ibid., 1:260; see also D&C 131:1–4).

4. Clark, *Behold the Lamb of God,* 64–65. It is unclear how Lucifer convinced a third part of the host of heaven to follow him. Were these individuals who did not "shout for joy" at the introduction of the plan by the Father? Were they afraid that they could not succeed? While we cannot say for sure, it seems highly unlikely that the Father would present the plan in such a way as to scare His children or to provoke in them feelings of despair because what was being proposed appeared impossible. The exact sophistry used by Lucifer to convince a portion to reject the Father's plan is unclear. But it is highly unlikely that the way the Father presented the plan left those present in a state of fear and doubt.

5. Roberts, *Comprehensive History,* 1:xxx.

6. As Elder Russell M. Nelson noted, "Knowingly we wanted the risks of mortality, which would allow the exercise of agency and accountability" ("Doors of Death," *Ensign,* May 1992, 72).

7. On a related note, some have assumed that the fact that a third part of the hosts of heaven fell from their first estate in the premortal world is evidence that the Father will lose *at least* 33 percent of His children. But this is a misreading of both history and scripture. The scriptures do not say that the Father lost one-third of His children. They do not say He lost 33 percent. Rather, they say a "third part" fell (Revelation 12:4; D&C 29:36). The difference may seem subtle, but it is real. Richard Draper wrote: "One-third, symbolically [shows] that their bounds have been set. They can go only so far. The fraction one-third is used by a number of the prophets in association with what is called 'remnant theology,' the remnant being the unaffected part. We see this in Ezekiel 5:1–5 . . . [and] again in Ezekiel 5:12 and in Zechariah 13:8–9" (*Opening the Seven Seals,* 95–96). In scripture, when the fraction one-third is used toward a particular individual or event, the suggestion is that they have a limited degree of power or influence (ibid., 108; Parry and Parry, *Understanding the Book of Revelation,* 110). Thus, in Revelation 8, John sees fire and desolation poured out upon the earth during the seventh seal but preceding the Second Coming (vv. 7–12). In this outpouring he views a "third part" of the trees and green grass burnt up; a "third part" of the sea turned to blood; a "third part" of the creatures in the sea and boats on the sea being destroyed; a "third part" of all water becoming bitter and undrinkable; and a "third part" of the sun, moon, and stars darkened. All of this, though catastrophic, nevertheless is intended to send the message that not "everything" is destroyed. God yet exhibits a degree of mercy by

limiting the power or influence of the disasters John was shown in his vision. When John speaks of the war in heaven, he states that the devil drew a "third part" of the hosts of heaven with him (Revelation 12:4; D&C 29:36). Again, the distinction between "one-third" and a "third part" may seem subtle, yet it is real. The fraction one-third implies 33 percent. The phrase "third part" implies a numerically undetermined segment of the population, who stand as a symbol that Satan's power over the premortal spirits was limited. Thus, the numerology in the passage implies that we have no knowledge of the fraction or percentage of Father's children who followed the adversary. All we know is that Satan had a limited influence over those in the presence of God. Hence, we should not assume that the Father has lost a significant number. The scriptures make no such point, and all such assumptions come from a misreading of the standard works of the Church.

8. Of Elder McConkie's conservative and mainstream approach, Robert L. Millet wrote: "Latter-day Saints who are at least distantly acquainted with his sermons and writings, who know him as one of the significant doctrinal voices of this dispensation, also know him to be one who is firm, steadfast, and straightforward in his declaration of the plan of salvation and of what it takes for men and women to be saved. Few of us would be prone to accuse him of being too loose, too lax, too liberal on the divinely established standards for peace and joy here and for exaltation in eternity" (*Within Reach,* 17).

9. Bruce R. McConkie, as cited in ibid., 10.

10. Bruce R. McConkie, as cited in ibid., 13–14.

11. McConkie, *Sermons and Writings,* 54.

12. McConkie, "Jesus Christ and Him Crucified," in *Speeches,* 400–401.

13. Bruce R. McConkie, as cited in Millet, *Within Reach,* 14.

14. Bruce R. McConkie, as cited in McConkie, Millet, and Top, *Doctrinal Commentary,* 4:95; Millet and McConkie, *Life Beyond,* 137; Millet, *Within Reach,* 12–13.

15. McConkie, "Seven Deadly Heresies," in *Charge to Religious Educators,* 149.

16. Millet, *Within Reach,* 18. Some have erroneously supposed that the 144,000 mentioned in the book of Revelation (see Revelation 7:4) consist of all who will be exalted in the celestial kingdom. But such is not the case. Whereas the number twelve symbolizes priesthood, the number 144,000—a multiple of

twelve—represents the fulness of the priesthood, or making one's calling and election sure. The number 144,000 serves to highlight the necessity of priesthood and priesthood ordinances (e.g., "twelve thousand" of each tribe) in our path to exaltation. It emphasizes that those who partake of the ordinances required by the Lord and then keep the covenants associated therewith shall become members of the Church of the Firstborn and have their calling and election made sure. This is available to *all* of God's children, not to a predetermined, limited number. Of this verse, one commentator wrote: "Twelve represents the priesthood. Biblical people squared a number to amplify its symbolic meaning. Thus, 144 suggests a fullness of priesthood authority. But John is not satisfied with that. He gives the image a superlative quality by multiplying 1,000, representing completeness. In this way he shows the strength and breadth of the priesthood in the latter days, in this dispensation that is, indeed, the dispensation of the fullness of times. During this period that complete priesthood authority will operate" (Draper, *Opening the Seven Seals,* 83). For additional information on the symbolic nature of the number 144,000, see Gaskill, *Lost Language of Symbolism,* 134–36, 321.

17. McConkie, Millet, and Top, *Doctrinal Commentary,* 4:94; emphasis added.

18. McConkie, *Answers,* 76–78.

19. Millet and McConkie, *Life Beyond,* 137. See also Millet, *Within Reach,* 1–13.

20. Robinson and Garrett, *Commentary,* 2:310.

21. McConkie and Ostler, *Revelations of the Restoration,* 533.

22. Elder McConkie argues that although very few people who are alive when Christ returns will be worthy to endure His presence and not be destroyed, nevertheless, during the Millennium, Satan will be bound and "children will grow up in an environment of righteousness" (*Millennial Messiah,* 651, 669). Thus, "those who live on the new [millennial] earth with its new heavens shall be saved" (ibid., 671). Statistically, Elder McConkie reasons, "More people will live on earth during the millennial era than in all the six millenniums that preceded it combined" (ibid., 671). Therefore, the majority of God's children will *not* be damned, or kept out of God's presence in the next life.

23. See Millet, *Within Reach,* 11.

24. Statistics gathered from the World Health Organization, *Human*

Development Reports, and the CIA's *World Fact Book.* See also reports in the Church periodical *The Contributor,* where we read: "The infant mortality on Ward Island, New York, is over ninety percent. Very nearly all die. And the result is the same in Boston, Philadelphia, London and Paris. The causes, in most instances, are hereditary syphilis and neglect" (Thatcher, "Mormon Polygamy and Christian Monogamy," 197). And: "If there is any field where the philanthropist and reformer is most urgently demanded, it is to limit the infant mortality which prevails to such an alarming extent in our great cities. In New York, Boston and Philadelphia, over one fourth, in Cincinnati nearly one third, of all the children born alive perish within the first year of life. What a portentous fact is this! What are the causes of this frightful mortality? We will mention one. A physician of wide experience has calculated, after careful inquiry, that fourth on the list of causes is hereditary syphilis. But even this statement does not at all convey an adequate idea of the effect of this disease on limiting and corrupting population. Of the infants which are still-born, the number is very great, and of these, the most frequent cause of death, according to that cautious writer, Berkeley Hill, is syphilis. But even if the child survives its first year, the danger is not past. It may be the picture of health till five or six years of age, or to the period of puberty, or even to adult age, and then first reveal the long concealed poison which has lurked in the system ever since its being began. That poison shows itself under a hundred protean forms. It may be in eruptions on the skin and foul ulcerations, or in obstinate 'colds in the head,' in swelling of the bones, in a peculiar affection of the eyes leading to blindness, in brittle and loose teeth, in the protean symptoms of scrofula, in idiocy, stunted growth, and in insanity. Such are the legacies which parents who, through vice or misfortune, have been cursed with this disease, have to hand down to their offspring. 'The fathers have eaten sour grapes and the children's teeth are set on edge'" (ibid., 162–63).

25. See Flinn, *European Demographic System,* 92, table 6.9.

26. See ibid., 17, table 2.2, and 94, table 6.10.

27. See Bagnall and Frier, *Demography of Roman Egypt,* 34–35.

28. Flinn, *European Demographic System,* 16.

29. Powell, *Status and Health in Prehistory,* 94–95. These statistics are estimates and are largely, although not exclusively, based on a sample of the Moundville Chiefdom of west central Alabama. They were a sedentary

agricultural people. Their society flourished in the five hundred years immediately preceding the European discovery of the New World. However, Dr. Powell does note that "the same pattern is evident in the mortality distributions reported . . . for a broad range of population samples" and by a large number of scholars specializing in the field of mortality rates. See ibid., 95.

30. Taylor, *Gospel Kingdom,* 119.

31. Smith, "Nephi's Descendants?" in *Review of Books on the Book of Mormon* 6, no. 1 (1994): 270–71.

32. Smith, *Doctrines of Salvation,* 2:53.

33. Ibid., 2:49–57. Elder Bruce R. McConkie expounded on this doctrine in his "Funeral Address for Rebecca Adams," his granddaughter, given 28 October 1967. Among other things, Elder McConkie taught the following: "Now I shall read a statement or two that the Prophet Joseph Smith has said about children who die before they arrive at the years of accountability. In part this applies to children generally, but in particular it applies to children who are born under the covenant who come into the lineage and house of Israel. He said: 'I have meditated upon the subject, and asked the question, why it is that infants, innocent children, are taken away from us, especially those that seem to be the most intelligent and interesting.' And then he answers the question, as it were, by giving the result of his meditation: 'The Lord takes many away, even in infancy, that they may escape the envy of man, and the sorrows and evils of this present world; they were too pure, too lovely, to live on earth; therefore, if rightly considered, instead of mourning we have reason to rejoice as they are delivered from evil, and we shall soon have them again.' (Joseph Smith, *Teachings of the Prophet Joseph Smith,* pp. 196–97.) Now in effect what that means is that there are certain spirits who come into this life only to receive bodies; for reasons that we do not know, but which are known in the infinite wisdom of the Eternal Father, they do not need the testing, probationary experiences of mortality. . . . Then the Prophet says: 'All children are redeemed by the blood of Jesus Christ, and the moment that children leave this world, they are taken to the bosom of Abraham [meaning, to the paradise of God]. The only difference between the old and young dying is, one lives longer in heaven and eternal light and glory than the other, and is freed a little sooner from this miserable wicked world. Notwithstanding all this glory, we for a moment lose sight of it, and mourn the loss, but we do not mourn as those without hope.' (*Teachings,* p. 197.) I read a

sermon by President John Taylor in which he was talking about little children who die before they arrive at the age of accountability, and the fact that they shall be saved, because of the atoning sacrifice of Christ, in the celestial kingdom of heaven. He made some calculations as to the percentage of mankind, who had died before they arrived at the years of accountability. His conclusion was that about one-half of those who had lived from the days of Adam to his day, had passed on to the spirit world and would be in this category who would be saved through the atonement of Christ without the testing, probationary experiences that most of us undergo. . . . When we view the over-all perspective and consider the tremendous hosts that God has called home, as it were, before they arrived at the testing period of life, we cannot escape the conclusion that there is a hand of destiny in it; that the hand of divine providence is governing; that Deity has allotted the spirits who are to come to this earth; that he has determined the time before appointed and the seasons when they will be born, and has even allotted the earth's surface to certain choice lineages who come from Abraham and Jacob. His hand is in all of this. . . . Now, implicit in this is the fact that he knows that certain do not need the severe testing that we adults need, and as a consequence he takes them to Abraham's bosom as soon as they have received bodies or shortly thereafter. This is somewhat the state that children will have during the millennium. Those that are born in that day, according to the revelation, will grow up without sin unto salvation, and as a consequence won't have the testing, probationary experiences that some of the rest of us are subject to. . . . Now here is another phrase that the Prophet said in his sermon. Speaking of these children he said: 'They will there [that is, in the next life] enjoy the fulness of that light, glory and intelligence, which is prepared in the celestial kingdom.' (*Teachings,* p. 200.) Now if a child goes to enjoy a fulness of that light, glory, and intelligence which is found in a celestial kingdom, that means that the child has eternal life; and eternal life, by definition, is to be like God, and have the fulness of salvation, and to continue living in the family unit. The Book of Mormon statement categorically says of children who die: 'little children . . . have eternal life.' (Mosiah 15:25.) Now this means that the family unit continues for them. And in due course all the necessary arrangements are made to give them the alliances and associations that they ought to have. Let me read two passages of scripture from the Inspired Version which tells us what is involved in the salvation of children. I shall read these in the light of the Prophet's vision in which he recorded, 'And I also beheld that all children who die before they arrive at the years of accountability, are saved in the celestial kingdom of heaven.' (*Teachings,* p. 107.) Well, this is the scriptural account: 'Take heed that ye despise not one of these little ones [Jesus is talking], for I say unto you, That in heaven their angels do always behold the face of my Father who is in heaven.' That is, they come from the celestial world where their spirits behold the face of God, and that shows the purity and cleanliness that they have. Then Jesus said, 'For the Son of Man is come to save that which was lost and to call sinners to repentance, but these little ones have no need of repentance, and I will save them.' (I. V. Matt. 18:10–11.) That is God's promise to children; in essence it is that those who die have no need for testing and for repentance. Then on a later occasion, also from the scriptural account, I read this: 'Then were there brought unto him little children, that he should put his hands on them and pray, And the disciples rebuked them, saying, There is no need [now notice what actually transpired—There is no need], for Jesus hath said, Such shall be saved.' (JST Matt. 19:13.) Actually what they were trying to do was save Jesus a burden of blessing children because he already taught them: 'such shall be saved!' Hence, they didn't need blessing in order to get saved. But Jesus said, 'Suffer little children to come unto me, and forbid them not, for of such is the kingdom of heaven.' (JST Matt. 19:14.)"

34. Smith and Sjodahl, *Doctrine and Covenants Commentary,* 469.

35. McConkie, *Millennial Messiah,* 661.

36. Smith, *Joseph F. Smith,* 129.

37. McConkie, *Millennial Messiah,* 661–62.

38. Maxwell, *"But for a Small Moment,"* 116.

39. Joseph Fielding Smith, address at the funeral of Richard L. Evans; as cited in McConkie and Ostler, *Revelations of the Restoration,* 960.

40. Kimball, *Teachings,* 37.

41. Kimball, *Faith Precedes the Miracle,* 103, 104, 105.

42. Benson, *Teachings,* 348. I express my appreciation to Dr. Richard Moore for bringing this quotation to my attention.

43. See McConkie, *Answers,* 75. Robert L. Millet wrote: "But what of the children who have died before the age of accountability—billions of little ones from the days of Adam to the time of the Second Coming, whom the scriptures

affirm are 'saved in the celestial kingdom of heaven' (D&C 137:10)?" (*Within Reach,* 11–12).

44. Maxwell, *"But for a Small Moment,"* 116.

45. Smith, *Doctrines of Salvation,* 2:55–56.

46. Ludlow et al., *Encyclopedia of Mormonism,* 2:715.

47. McConkie, *New Witness,* 643.

48. McConkie, Millet, and Top, *Doctrinal Commentary,* 4:94–95. See also Millet and McConkie, *Life Beyond,* 136–37; Millet, *Within Reach,* 11–13.

49. McConkie, *Millennial Messiah,* 671. Elder McConkie also penned this: "During the millennium . . . death as we know it cannot intervene to cause a separation of body and spirit.

"'There shall be no more thence,' the Lord said to Isaiah, 'an infant of days, nor an old man that hath not filled his days: for *the child shall die an hundred years old;* but the sinner being an hundred years old shall be accursed.' (Isa. 65:20.)

"In our day the Lord has revealed: 'And there shall be no sorrow because *there is no death.* In that day *an infant shall not die until he is old;* and his life shall be as the age of a tree; And *when he dies* he shall not sleep, that is to say in the earth, but shall be changed in the twinkling of an eye, and shall be caught up, and his rest shall be glorious.' (D&C 101:29–31.)" (*Mormon Doctrine,* 497–98, s.v. "Millennium"; emphasis in original).

50. McConkie, *Doctrinal New Testament Commentary,* 3:475–76. Elsewhere he wrote: "However, Satan shall be bound (D&C 43:31; 45:55; 84:100; 88:110–111; Rev. 20:1–3, 7), and for a thousand years he 'shall not have power to tempt any man.' (D&C 101:28.) Accordingly, 'children shall grow up without sin unto salvation' (D&C 45:58), and righteousness and peace be everywhere present" (McConkie, *Doctrinal New Testament Commentary,* 3:570).

51. See McConkie, *Mormon Doctrine,* 804, s.v. "Translated Beings."

52. Millet, *Within Reach,* 11–13. See also McConkie, Millet, and Top, *Doctrinal Commentary,* 4:94–95; Millet and McConkie, *Life Beyond,* 136–37.

53. Elder Melvin J. Ballard once conjectured: "It is my judgment that any man or woman can do more to conform to the laws of God in one year in this life than they could in ten years when they are dead" (Hinckley, *Sermons and Missionary Services of Melvin Joseph Ballard,* 241). Perhaps this comment and others like it have been interpreted to imply that acceptance of the gospel in the

spirit world is "ten times harder" than acceptance of it on the earth—although Elder Ballard makes no such statement here. Similarly, Oliver B. Huntington quoted the Prophet Joseph Smith as having said that we should improve ourselves while we are here in mortality, for "a man can do as much in this life in one year as he can do in ten years in the spirit world without the body" (Huntington, "Sayings of Joseph Smith," *Young Woman's Journal* 2, no. 8 [May 1891]: 366). Notice, like the quotation by Elder Ballard, Joseph does not say that it is "ten times harder" to accept the gospel in the spirit world. Rather, he suggests that it is ten times harder to function without a body in the spirit world. Nonetheless, such comments, misinterpreted, appear to be the source for the idea that acceptance of the gospel in the spirit world is much more difficult than it is in mortality.

54. Elder Neal A. Maxwell penned this: "Of the approximately 70 billion individuals who, up to now, have inhabited this planet, probably not more than one percent have really heard the gospel. Today no more than one-tenth of one percent of the world's population are members of the Church. Even so, before the final judgment and resurrection *all* will have had an adequate opportunity to hear the gospel of Jesus Christ. This underscores the mercy of God and the justice of God. (See D&C 1:2)." (*"But for a Small Moment,"* 115–16; emphasis in original).

55. One historian noted: "Lorenzo Snow and [Wilford] Woodruff both agreed that 'very few of those who die without the Gospel will reject it on the other side of the vail'" (Alexander, *Things in Heaven and Earth,* 322). See also Parry and Parry, *Understanding Death and the Resurrection,* 110–11.

56. Woodruff, in Stuy, *Collected Discourses,* 4:74. President Woodruff went on to say: "Jesus . . . went and preached to the spirits in prison, who were destroyed in the days of Noah. . . . [T]hey doubtless gladly embraced the Gospel, and . . . will be saved in the kingdom of God. The fathers of this people will embrace the Gospel [too]. . . . Brethren and sisters, lay these things to heart. . . . Great and glorious are these principles which God has revealed to us concerning the redemption of our dead. I tell you when the prophets and apostles go to preach to those who are shut up in prison, and who have not received the Gospel, thousands of them will there embrace the Gospel. They know more in that world than they do here" (ibid., 4:74, 75, 76). See also Packer, *Holy Temple,* 203, 206; Millet, *Within Reach,* 12–13.

57. Smith, in Conference Report, Apr. 1962, 66.

58. Lund, in Conference Report, Oct. 1903, 82.

59. Smith, *Doctrines of Salvation,* 2:133.

60. Smith, in Conference Report, Apr. 1908, 25.

61. Snow, in Stuy, *Collected Discourses,* 3:363.

62. Woodbury, "This Person Has Accepted the Gospel," 19, as cited in Jensen, *When Faith Writes the Story,* 224, or in Calhoun, *When Faith Writes the Story,* 241.

63. See, for example, McConkie, Millet, and Top, *Doctrinal Commentary,* 4:94–95; Millet and McConkie, *Life Beyond,* 136–37; Millet, *Within Reach,* 11–13.

64. Woodruff, in Stuy, *Collected Discourses,* 4:74, 75, 76. See also Packer, *Holy Temple,* 203, 206; Millet, *Within Reach,* 12–13.

65. Though one source argues that "accepting the gospel, of course, does not equate with entering the celestial kingdom" (Parry and Parry, *Understanding Death and Resurrection,* 113), I'm inclined to take issue with this reasoning. True, "every knee shall bow, and every tongue confess" that Jesus is the Christ (Mosiah 27:31)—and simply accepting the gospel does not ensure exaltation. However, in the various talks I have cited, none of the Brethren were speaking about individuals who would accept the gospel in the spirit world for a place in the terrestrial or telestial kingdom. On the contrary, the context of every one of the quotations was a belief that the large number of individuals accepting the gospel would then be exalted. Thus, for example, President Wilford Woodruff speaks of "fifty thousand millions" waiting to hear the gospel in the spirit world. Then he says that as they hear the elders' testimonies (in the spirit world) and accept their message, we will "attend to the ordinances of the house of God for them" and they will then "come forth in the morning of the first resurrection and have a part therein with us" (in *Journal of Discourses,* 16:269). Clearly President Woodruff saw these as people who would be exalted, not simply redeemed from spirit prison. [Similarly, Patriarch Eldred G. Smith's comment was followed by the acknowledgment that God has prepared "valiant spirits" to "assist those who have accepted the gospel in the spirit world."] Assist them to do what? Why, to have the ordinances necessary for exaltation. And why would we do ordinances for them if they had accepted the gospel but we knew they were not going to be exalted? As President Joseph Fielding Smith noted, the

only people who need ordinances performed for them are those who will go to the celestial kingdom (see *Doctrines of Salvation,* 2:329). Thus, if we are performing ordinances for those we know have accepted the gospel in the spirit world, this clearly implies that Patriarch Smith saw these as people who were going to be eternal residents of the celestial kingdom. In addition, statements by the presiding Brethren say that an incomprehensibly large number will be exalted. (See the discussion at the beginning of this chapter.) Yet, since the numbers of those who enjoy the blessing of having the fulness of the gospel during mortality are comparatively few, we know most of those found in the celestial kingdom are individuals who accepted the truth on the other side of the veil. Thus, apparently a very large percentage of those who hear the truth in the spirit world also accept it and are rewarded a place in the highest degree of the celestial kingdom. So, though it is true that *some* will reject the gospel in the spirit world, nevertheless, it appears to me that the vast majority who accept it in the spirit world will then receive their exaltations.

Chapter Three: The Doctrine of Sanctification

1. Brewster, *Doctrine and Covenants Encyclopedia,* s.v. "Justification."
2. Colin B. Douglas, "Justification," in Ludlow et al., *Encyclopedia of Mormonism,* 2:776.
3. McConkie, *Mormon Doctrine,* 408, s.v. "Justification."
4. C. Eric Ott, "Sanctification," in Ludlow et al., *Encyclopedia of Mormonism,* 3:1259; McConkie, *Mormon Doctrine,* 675, s.v. "Sanctification."
5. Smith, *Teachings,* 314, 360.
6. McConkie, *New Witness,* 290.
7. Ibid., 244. See also McConkie, *Sermons and Writings,* 349; *Millennial Messiah,* 536; *Mormon Doctrine,* 70, s.v. "Baptism."
8. McConkie, *New Witness,* 239.
9. Eyring, "Gifts of the Spirit for Hard Times," 4.
10. Christofferson, "Justification and Sanctification," *Ensign,* June 2001, 23.
11. The prayer on the water is as follows: "O God, the Eternal Father, we ask thee in the name of thy Son, Jesus Christ, to bless and sanctify this [water] to the souls of all those who drink of it, that they may do it in remembrance of the blood

of thy Son, which was shed for them; that they may witness unto thee, O God, the Eternal Father, that they do always remember him, that they may have his Spirit to be with them. Amen" (D&C 20:79; see also Moroni 5:2).

12. McConkie, *New Witness,* 299.

13. Additionally, an eight-year-old being baptized should not be told that he or she is now "the cleanest person in the room," as it implies that prior to baptism the child was "dirty" or sinful. And we know that children prior to the age of eight have no sins (see Moroni 8:10–15).

14. McConkie, *Mortal Messiah,* 3:41, n. 1.

15. Joseph Smith to Brigham Young, in Watson, *Manuscript History of Brigham Young,* 529. See also Romney, in Conference Report, Apr. 1944, 140–41; Faust, in Conference Report, Apr. 1989, 42; Bednar, "That We May Always Have His Spirit to Be with Us," *Ensign,* May 2006, 31.

16. See Jensen, "Have I Received an Answer from the Spirit?" *Ensign,* Apr. 1989, 21–25.

17. Smith, *Teachings,* 148.

18. Young, in *Journal of Discourses,* 8:124.

19. McConkie, *Mormon Doctrine,* 675, s.v. "Sanctification."

20. Clarke, "'Hold Up Your Light,'" *Ensign,* May 1985, 74. See also Clarke, "Be a Witness of God," *Church News,* 14 Apr. 1985, 21. Elder Neal A. Maxwell once noted: "Even if we decide to leave Babylon, some of us endeavor to keep a second residence there, or we commute on weekends" (*Wonderful Flood of Light,* 47).

21. McConkie, *Mortal Messiah,* 3:41, n. 1.

Chapter Four: Vicarious Work for the Dead

1. Of course, by "destroyed" Malachi means damned, or kept from residing eternally in the presence of God.

2. Madsen, *Joseph Smith the Prophet,* 51–65.

3. See Ankerberg and Weldon, *Behind the Mask,* 52.

4. Decker, *Complete Handbook on Mormonism,* 268–69; emphasis added.

5. Maxwell, *"But for a Small Moment,"* 115.

6. In a similar spirit, one Evangelical Christian website (www.fewtherebe.com) makes this declaration: "Most people will never make it to Heaven.

I realize that this sounds like a pretty obnoxious idea to most people. Nevertheless, it is certainly the truth. Most people will decide to reject Jesus and spend eternity in Hell rather than to trust Jesus and go to Heaven when they die."

7. See 1 Peter 3:18–19 and commentary on this passage in Marshall, *1 Peter,* 122–23; Reicke, *Epistles of James, Peter, and Jude,* 111; Davids, *First Epistle of Peter,* 138. See also 1 Peter 4:6 and commentary on this verse in Elliott, *1 Peter,* 733; Reicke, *Epistles of James, Peter, and Jude,* 119; Davids, *First Epistle of Peter,* 153; Theophylact, "Commentary on 1 Peter," in Bray, *James, 1–2 Peter, 1–3 John, Jude,* 114; Hilary, "Introductory Commentary on 1 Peter," in ibid., 113; Oecumenisu, "Commentary on I Peter," in ibid., 114.

8. See Hippolytus, "Against Plato, on the Cause of the Universe," in Roberts and Donaldson, *Ante-Nicene Fathers,* 5:221–22; Tertullian, "On the Soul," in Bray, *James, 1–2 Peter, 1–3 John, Jude,* 107; Origen, "Against Celsus," bk. 2, chap. 43, in Roberts and Donaldson, *Ante-Nicene Fathers,* 4:448; Kelly, *Early Christian Doctrines,* 472; Cyril of Alexandria, "Catena," in Bray, *James, 1–2 Peter, 1–3 John, Jude,* 107, 108; Severus, "Catena," in ibid., 108; Ammonius, "Catena," in ibid., 108; Irenaeus, "Against Heresies," bk. 4, chap. 27, v. 2, in Roberts and Donaldson, *Ante-Nicene Fathers,* 1:403, 499; Justin Martyr, "Dialogue with Trypho," chap. 72, in ibid., 1:235; "The Pastor of Hermas," bk. 3, sim. 9, chap. 16, in ibid., 2:49; Tertullian, "A Treatise on the Soul," in ibid., 3:231, 234–35.

9. Although baptism for the dead is not the only vicarious ordinance, it is the one most clearly attested to in scripture (see 1 Corinthians 15:29). And though this ordinance tends to conjure up strange images in the minds of non-Latter-day Saints, nonetheless biblical scholars not of our faith acknowledge its validity based on the Bible. See, for example, Conybeare and Howson, *Life and Epistles of St. Paul,* 412–13; Orr and Walther, *1 Corinthians,* 337; Nicoll, *Expositor's Greek Testament,* 2:930; Murphy-O'Connor, "The First Letter to the Corinthians," in Brown, Fitzmyer, and Murphy, *New Jerome Biblical Commentary,* 813, n. 70; Ellis, *Seven Pauline Letters,* 110; Dummelow, *One-Volume Bible Commentary,* 919; Morris, *1 Corinthians,* 214, 215; Mare, "1 Corinthians," in Gaebelein, *Expositor's Bible Commentary,* 10:287; Ambrosiaster, "Commentary on Paul's Epistles," in Bray, *1–2 Corinthians,* 166; Epiphanius, "Against Heresies," in Nibley, *Mormonism and Early Christianity,* 125–26. See also Roberts, *Gospel,* 246–47.

10. See Smith, *Doctrines of Salvation,* 2:164. See also Smith, *Answers to Gospel Questions,* 4:165.

Chapter Five: What of the "Strait and Narrow Path"?

1. See, for example, McConkie, *Doctrinal New Testament Commentary,* 3:476–77; McConkie *Answers,* 76–77; McConkie, Millet, and Top, *Doctrinal Commentary,* 4:94–95; Millet and McConkie, *Life Beyond,* 136–37; Romney, "Worth of Souls," *Ensign,* Nov. 1978, 14–15.

2. On a related note, in the April 2004 general conference of the Church, Elder Dallin H. Oaks gave a talk entitled "Preparation for the Second Coming." The theme of Elder Oaks's remarks was summarized by a statement at the beginning of his talk: "If we are prepared we need not fear (see D&C 38:30)" (*Ensign,* May 2004, 7). Elder Oaks went on to speak about the importance of studying the signs of the times in order that we might be prepared for Christ's return. As a warning about the dangers of this fallen world and the importance of being prepared for the Lord's return, Elder Oaks cited the parable of the ten virgins and then stated: "The arithmetic of this parable is chilling. The ten virgins obviously represent members of Christ's Church, for all were invited to the wedding feast and all knew what was required to be admitted when the bridegroom came. But only half were ready when he came." He went on to say: "Not surprisingly, many of our youth and adults are caught up in pornography, pagan piercing of body parts, self-serving pleasure pursuits, dishonest behavior, revealing attire, foul language, and degrading sexual indulgence. . . . Many also deny individual responsibility and practice dependence on others, seeking, like the foolish virgins, to live on borrowed substance and borrowed light." Some have taken Elder Oaks's remarks in this talk as an apostolic declaration that 50 percent of Latter-day Saints will be damned. However, it should be noted that Elder Oaks made no such claim. While he did say that the parable of the ten virgins' representation of five prepared and five unprepared members was "chilling," he did not say that this was some sort of mathematical prediction. Rather, Elder Oaks was suggesting that the parable is a warning that *not* everyone invited to the wedding feast is going to be admitted—and we have the ability to ensure that we are not among the "foolish virgins" who are shut out. Some may wonder why the parable speaks of "ten" virgins—with five wise and five foolish—if

this is not a numeric prediction. Readers should be aware that parables are not the same as allegories. One crucial difference between the two is the extent to which their details are symbolic. With allegories, often most of the details have significance and require interpretation. With parables, however, taking the interpretation too far will do damage to the parable and no doubt confuse the recipient. A good example may be found in the parables of the unjust judge (see Luke 18:1–8) and the friend at midnight (see Luke 11:5–13). In both of these parables we see a male figure, which, if taken as a representation of God the Father, completely distorts the intended message. Similarly, it is quite possible that we are not intended to interpret the ten virgins, or the five and five, as anything more than a group. We know that anciently the number ten denoted "the whole of a part," or part of the whole, but not the whole itself (Draper, *Opening the Seven Seals,* 123–24, 132, 164; see also Parry and Parry, *Understanding the Book of Revelation,* 229). In other words, if the numbers in the parable of the ten virgins were intended to be interpreted, then they may simply represent a whole or complete unit that exists within a greater whole. In this view, they may represent a segment of the Church's membership—but not the membership as a whole. And what would that segment which they represent be? They may symbolize the practicing or active Saints—hence they are referred to as "virgins." In this view, they are members of the Church with a certain level of purity. They are *probably* temple recommend holders with ethical lifestyles and a testimony of the restored gospel. Notice in the parable they are *all* awaiting the bridegroom. They *all* have lamps. They are *all* depicted as wanting to do what is right. Thus, they may be symbols of that portion of the Church that seeks to do God's will but which, in the end, does not *all* succeed—or does not endure to the end. From another perspective, the number five is highlighted in the parable. If that number was intended as symbolic, we might rightfully ask ourselves what it symbolizes. Although not a common number in scriptural symbolism, two ideas are associated with the number five: God's grace, and man in his fallen state (see Gaskill, *Lost Language of Symbolism,* 120–22). One commentator argued that in the parable of the ten virgins (see Matthew 25:1–13) the number five is used as a symbol for both God's grace and the nature of fallen man (see Johnston, *Numbers in the Bible,* 64–66). In this model, the five wise virgins who have oil in their lamps—or testimonies and righteousness in their hearts—would be a representation of the grace of God, or those who will receive of God's grace at the judgment bar. The five unwise virgins, of course, represent those who, in the spirit of fallen man as an "enemy" to God (Mosiah 3:19), have not prepared themselves for the coming of Christ. It is their fallen nature that keeps them from being fully prepared to meet the Savior when he comes. Thus, if we are to examine the numbers from the perspective of scriptural symbolism, we may conclude that this parable is not telling us which fraction will be damned and which will be saved. On the contrary, it is telling us *how* one group will be saved and another will be damned. The message is about grace versus fallen humanity—and not about what fraction of God's children will be saved. In the end, we cannot say for sure what exactly Matthew intended you and me to understand by the numbers five and ten in the parable of the ten virgins. However, a modern apostolic witness has suggested the message is primarily a general warning and not a statistical analysis of how many will be damned.

3. Ogden and Skinner, *Four Gospels,* 221.

4. McConkie, *Doctrinal New Testament Commentary,* 1:250.

5. This rephrasing of the verse comes from Dr. Richard G. Moore.

6. McConkie, *Doctrinal New Testament Commentary,* 1:495–96.

7. Regarding how God treats those who do not know of the truth while in mortality, the Prophet Joseph Smith taught: "To say that the heathens would be damned because they did not believe the Gospel would be preposterous, and to say that the Jews would all be damned that do not believe in Jesus would be equally absurd; for 'how can they believe on him of whom they have not heard, and how can they hear without a preacher, and how can he preach except he be sent;' consequently neither Jew nor heathen can be culpable for rejecting the conflicting opinions of sectarianism, nor for rejecting any testimony but that which is sent of God, for as the preacher cannot preach except he be sent, so the hearer cannot believe without he hear a 'sent' preacher, and cannot be condemned for what he has not heard, and being without law, will have to be judged without law" (*Teachings,* 221). The Prophet Joseph also stated: "We are frequently asked the question, what has become of our fathers? Will they all be damned for not obeying the Gospel, when they never heard it? Certainly not. But they will possess the same privilege that we here enjoy, through the medium of the everlasting Priesthood, which not only administers on earth, but also in heaven" (ibid., 221–22). On another occasion, he added: "The Great Parent of

the universe looks upon the whole of the human family . . . as His offspring, and . . . will judge all men, 'not according to the narrow, contracted notions of men, but, according to the deeds done in the body whether they be good or evil.' . . . Those who have lived without law, will be judged without law" (ibid., 218). And finally, he taught: "It is an opinion which is generally received, that the destiny of man is irretrievably fixed at his death, and that he is made either eternally happy, or eternally miserable; that if a man dies without a knowledge of God, he must be eternally damned, without any mitigation of his punishment, alleviation of his pain, or the most latent hope of a deliverance while endless ages shall roll along. However orthodox this principle may be, we shall find that it is at variance with the testimony of Holy Writ" (ibid., 218–19).

8. Unfortunately, this type of experience is not all that uncommon. Dr. Richard G. Moore shared the following experience: "Shortly after my mission I worked with a guy at BYU who one day said, 'I feel sorry for all the people who closed the door on us as missionaries.' I would have thought that he should have felt sorry for them because they missed an opportunity to receive the gospel, but I knew this guy—so I asked, 'Why?' He responded, 'They had their chance!' I asked him what he meant. He said, 'Everyone gets a chance to hear the gospel, and they had their chance.' 'So,' I said, 'here is a lady in her home, crying baby in her arm, dinner boiling over on the stove, phone ringing, and the Mormon missionaries knock at her door. She opens the door, sees who it is, and says, *I'm sorry; I just can't be bothered right now.* You're telling me that she had her chance to hear the gospel?' 'Yes,' he said, 'that was her chance and she missed it. The gospel is more important than any other thing that was happening in her life.' 'But she didn't know that,' I said. 'Well, she should have found out. She's had her chance!' he said."

9. Bruce R. McConkie, as cited in Millet, *Within Reach,* 10. See also McConkie, Millet, and Top, *Doctrinal Commentary,* 4:94–95; McConkie, *Answers,* 76–78; Millet and McConkie, *Life Beyond,* 136–37.

10. McConkie, *Doctrinal New Testament Commentary,* 3:477.

11. McConkie, Millet, and Top, *Doctrinal Commentary,* 4:94–95. See also Millet and McConkie, *Life Beyond,* 136–37.

12. McConkie, *Answers,* 76, 77.

13. See Millet, "The House of Israel: From Everlasting to Everlasting," in

Draper, *Witness of Jesus Christ,* 179; Matthews, "Role of the House of Israel"; Millet and McConkie, *Our Destiny.*

14. See Millet, "House of Israel," in Draper, *Witness of Jesus Christ,* 178–99.

15. Nelson, "Tender Roots Need Strength," in *Church News,* 14 Apr. 1985, 5; see also Whitney, *Saturday Night Thoughts,* 133; McConkie, *Mormon Doctrine,* 81, s.v. "Believing Blood."

16. See McConkie, *New Witness,* 34.

17. Ogden and Skinner, *Four Gospels,* 221.

18. McConkie, Millet, and Top, *Doctrinal Commentary,* 4:93.

19. It may be wise here to reiterate a point about the 144,000 which John the Revelator speaks of as standing "before the throne, and before the Lamb, clothed with white robes" (Revelation 7:9). In scripture, the number twelve symbolizes priesthood: priesthood authority, priesthood power, and priesthood ordinances (see Gaskill, *Lost Language of Symbolism,* 134–36). Multiples of twelve, therefore, are traditionally understood to be a symbol for the "fullness of the priesthood" or making one's calling and election sure (Smith, *Book of Revelation,* 48; Draper, *Opening the Seven Seals,* 46, 83, 156). Thus, one commentary notes, "Anytime the number 12 is multiplied by another number, it symbolizes an increase in power and covenant responsibility" (Smith, *Book of Revelation,* 288–89). So in Revelation 7:4 we read, "And I heard the number of them which were sealed: and there were sealed an hundred and forty and four thousand of all the tribes of the children of Israel." Of these 144,000 individuals, the Lord has stated, "We are to understand that those who are sealed are high priests, ordained unto the holy order of God, to administer the everlasting gospel; for they are they who are ordained out of every nation, kindred, tongue, and people, by the angels to whom is given power over the nations of the earth, to bring as many as will come to the church of the Firstborn" (D&C 77:11). Clearly this number is not intended to be taken as literal. Rather, it serves to highlight the necessity of priesthood and priesthood ordinances for all of God's children, e.g., "twelve thousand" of each tribe. It emphasizes the fact that those who partake of the ordinances required by the Lord and then keep the covenants associated therewith shall become members of the Church of the Firstborn and have their calling and election made sure. This is available to *all* of God's children, *not* to a predetermined, limited number. Substantiation that this is intended as a symbolic number can be found in the fact that the list of the twelve tribes from which

the 144,000 are to be drawn varies in different passages of scripture. For example, the 12,000 members of the tribe of Dan are sometimes listed as being part of the 144,000 (see Exodus 1:1–4; Deuteronomy 27:12–13; 1 Chronicles 2:1–2; Ezekiel 48:1–7, 23–28). At other times, however, Dan is dropped from the list (see Revelation 7:5–8), and 12,000 members of the tribe of Manasseh are plugged in to replace Dan—implying that God will draw part of the 144,000 from that tribe instead of from the tribe of Dan. Thus, clearly the 144,000 are a symbolic number representing *all* who will be exalted. It does not literally imply that God will exalt 12,000 from each of the twelve tribes.

20. See Eyring, "Gifts of the Spirit for Hard Times," 1–6.

21. In responding to this comment and the seeming disparities of life, a colleague of mine made the following comment: "If anything, I feel I am 'over-blessed'! How can it be just for me to receive all I do, when there are so many who do not even comprehend what they are missing? Not just some things, but everything! Glory be to the Father and the Son forever and ever, worlds without end!"

Chapter Six: When a Loved One Strays

1. Whitney, *Life of Heber C. Kimball,* 450.
2. Hinckley, *Teachings,* 410.
3. Ibid., 412.
4. Ibid., 413.
5. Ibid., 410.
6. Ibid., 413.
7. Hinckley, "Let Not Your Heart Be Troubled," in *Speeches of the Year, 1974,* 269, 273.
8. In the Joseph Smith Translation of Matthew 7:1–5 we read: "Now these are the words which Jesus taught his disciples that they should say unto the people. Judge not unrighteously, that ye be not judged: but judge righteous judgment. For with what judgment ye judge, ye shall be judged: and with what measure ye mete, it shall be measured to you again. And again, ye shall say unto them, Why is it that thou beholdest the mote that is in thy brother's eye, but considerest not the beam that is in thine own eye? Or how wilt thou say to thy brother, Let me pull out the mote out of thine eye; and canst not behold a beam in thine own eye?"

9. For example, in Psalm 44:20–21 we read: "If we have forgotten the name of our God, or stretched out our hands to a strange god; shall not God search this out? for he knoweth the secrets of the heart." Proverbs 21:2 states: "Every way of a man is right in his own eyes: but the Lord pondereth the hearts." Jeremiah 11:20 informs us: "But, O Lord of hosts, that judgest righteously, that triest the reins and the heart." In Mormon 8:19 the following appears: "For behold, the same that judgeth rashly shall be judged rashly again; for according to his works shall his wages be; therefore, he that smiteth shall be smitten again, of the Lord." In Psalm 19:19 we find this: "The judgments of the Lord are true and righteous altogether." Again, from John we read: "Lord God Almighty, true and righteous are thy judgments" (Revelation 16:7). In Hebrews 4:12 we are told: "For the word of God is . . . a discerner of the thoughts and intents of the heart."

10. Hinckley, *Teachings,* 412.

11. Maxwell, "Old Testament," 17.

12. See *Webster's 1806 Dictionary,* 297. See also *Random House Webster's College Dictionary* (1996), 1331, s.v. "Succor."

13. Maxwell, "Old Testament," 17.

14. The Prophet Joseph Smith put it this way: "God dwells in eternity, and does not view things as we do" (*Teachings,* 356).

15. Brown, *Death of the Messiah,* 2:973.

16. Smith, *History of The Church of Jesus Christ of Latter-day Saints,* 5:530.

17. Ehat and Cook, *Words of Joseph Smith,* 241.

18. Whitney, in Conference Report, Apr. 1929, 110. Elder Orson F. Whitney was born in 1855, some eleven years after the Prophet Joseph was martyred. Thus, clearly he did not hear Joseph say these words. Where Elder Whitney learned them is uncertain, although he was a member of the Twelve when he shared them. Brigham Young University's Joseph Fielding McConkie wrote the following about Elder Whitney's comments (as they were quoted in "Hope for Parents of Wayward Children," *Ensign,* Sep. 2002, 11): "The question then becomes where did Brother Whitney get the ideas he is presenting? A careful search of all that we have recorded from the Prophet reveals only one discourse in which he speaks about the matter. This is a talk given on 13 August 1843. It was a funeral discourse for Elias Higbee. Willard Richards recorded the discourse. He rendered the key sentence as follows: 'When a seal is put upon

the father and mother, it secures their posterity, so that they cannot be lost, but will be saved by virtue of the covenant of their father and mother.' (See *History of the Church,* 5:530.) Howard Cory, who had often been a scribe for the Prophet, also recorded the talk. He rendered the key sentence as follows: 'A measure of this sealing is to confirm upon their head in common with Elijah the doctrine of election or the covenant with Abraham—which when a Father & mother of a family have entered into['] their children who have not transgressed are secured by the seal wherewith the Parents have been sealed' ([Ehat and Cook,] *Words of Joseph Smith,* 241). Howard Cory is clearly making this promise conditional. Both accounts of the talk place this promise in the context of those parents who have 'made their calling and election sure.' This is quite a different matter than their simply having been married in the temple" (Letter to Richard Kempton, 2 Oct. 2002; used by permission).

Brother McConkie's point is that parents who will experience the fulfillment of Joseph's promise must first save themselves. No mother or father who falls short of exaltation can expect to somehow save his or her wayward child. However, as I believe and this book points out, a significantly high number of parents will be exalted. Thus, the Prophet Joseph's promise should not be looked upon with skepticism.

19. Young, in *Journal of Discourses,* 11:215. "Hope for Parents of Wayward Children" (*Ensign,* Sep. 2002, 11) draws this quotation from Smith, *Doctrines of Salvation,* 2:90–91.

20. Snow, in Stuy, *Collected Discourses,* 3:364. Notice that President Snow makes the same basic point the Prophet Joseph did, namely, that a father and mother must first secure their exaltation and then the blessings regarding their posterity may be claimed.

21. Packer, "Our Moral Environment," *Ensign,* May 1992, 68.

22. I say "Church-approved" in that its presence in the *Ensign*—an official periodical of The Church of Jesus Christ of Latter-day Saints—implies that the statement was approved by the Church Correlation Committee. Thus, we must assume that its contents contain sound doctrine. Indeed, the very fact that two presidents of the Church and two apostles are being quoted should, itself, be sufficient to establish the orthodoxy of the article.

23. See President Wilford Woodruff's comments delivered at the October 1890 general conference of the Church, in which he stated: "The Lord will

never permit me or any other man who stands as President of this Church to lead you astray. It is not in the programme. It is not in the mind of God. If I were to attempt that, the Lord would remove me out of my place, and so He will any other man who attempts to lead the children of men astray from the oracles of God and from their duty" ("Remarks by President George Q. Cannon and President Wilford Woodruff," *Deseret Evening News,* 11 Oct. 1890). See also "Excerpts from Three Addresses by President Wilford Woodruff Regarding the Manifesto," Doctrine and Covenants, 292.

24. Joseph Fielding McConkie to Gaskill, personal correspondence, 2 Oct. 2002. Copy in possession of the author.

25. McConkie, *Answers,* 73–74.

26. I've always found curious this statement by the Prophet Joseph Smith: "Except a man and his wife enter into an everlasting covenant and be married for eternity, while in this probation, by the power and authority of the Holy Priesthood, they will cease to increase when they die. . . . But those who are married by the power and authority of the priesthood in this life, and continue without committing the sin against the Holy Ghost, will continue to increase and have children in the celestial glory" (*Teachings,* 300–301). The Prophet speaks of the effect of a sealing upon a husband and wife who do not deny the Holy Ghost and thereby become sons and daughters of perdition. It is noteworthy that he explicitly promises those sealed in the temple that they will be gods, so long as they do not commit the unpardonable sin. All others who enter into the new and everlasting covenant of marriage, he implies, will be exalted.

27. Whitney, in Conference Report, Apr. 1929, 110.

28. Smith, *Teachings,* 321.

29. Ibid., 320, 321.

Chapter Seven: Conclusion

1. Robinson, *Believing Christ,* 78.

2. Elder Neal A. Maxwell wrote: "'And because of the simpleness of the way, or the easiness of it, there were many who perished.' (1 Nephi 17:41.) It is true today; the simpleness, the easiness of the gospel is such that it causes people to perish because they can't receive it. We like variety. We like intellectual embroidery. We like complexity. We like complexity at times because it

gives us an excuse for failure; that is, as you increase the complexity of a belief system, you provide more and more refuges for those who don't want to comply. You thereby increase the number of excuses that people can make for failure to comply, and you create a sophisticated intellectual structure which causes people to talk about the gospel instead of doing it. But the gospel of Jesus Christ really is not complex. It strips us of any basic excuse for noncompliance, and yet many of us are forever trying to make it more complex.

"The Book of Mormon suggests a third reason why we may like complexity and reject simplicity, and that is because complexity is pleasing to the carnal mind. It gives us sanctuaries for sin. There are other reasons for craving complexity. One is our simple lack of courage in facing our own deficiencies. The Book of Mormon uses this terse phrase: ' . . . The guilty taketh the truth to be hard, for it cutteth them to the very center.' (1 Nephi 16:2.)

"Most of us don't like to be cut to the center, and when the gospel standards cut us it hurts. The tendency is to deal with the pain by rejecting the surgery" ("*For the Power Is in Them . . . ,*" 48–49).

3. Teasdale, in Stuy, *Collected Discourses,* 4:40.

4. Young, in *Journal of Discourses,* 9:125.

5. Young, *Discourses,* 86. President Young also stated: "The plan by which God works is rational. . . . None will be destroyed except those who receive the oracles of truth and reject them. None are condemned except those who have the privilege of receiving the words of eternal life and refuse to receive them" (ibid., 58).

6. Maxwell, *Deposition of a Disciple,* 12.

7. Smith, *Teachings,* 240–41. In Galbraith's *Scriptural Teachings of the Prophet Joseph Smith,* the cross-references to this declaration by the Prophet include the following: Jacob 7:12, which reads: "And this is not all—it has been made manifest unto me, for I have heard and seen; and it also has been made manifest unto me by the power of the Holy Ghost; wherefore, I know if there should be no atonement made all mankind must be lost." Also, Mosiah 13:28, where we read: "And moreover, I say unto you, that salvation doth not come by the law alone; and were it not for the atonement, which God himself shall make for the sins and iniquities of his people, that they must unavoidably perish, notwithstanding the law of Moses." Finally, Galbraith cites Alma 34:9, which informs us: "For it is expedient that an atonement should be made; for according to the great plan of the Eternal God there must be an atonement made, or

else all mankind must unavoidably perish; yea, all are hardened; yea, all are fallen and are lost, and must perish except it be through the atonement which it is expedient should be made." Thus, according to Galbraith, Joseph is not saying *we* must make allowances for those who sin but that rather God makes allowances for man's weaknesses and shortcomings (see Galbraith, *Scriptural Teachings of the Prophet Joseph Smith,* 270, n. 5).

8. Coffin, "Sermon."

9. Smith, *Teachings,* 257.

10. Clark, in Conference Report, Oct. 1953, 84.

11. Whitney, in Conference Report, Apr. 1929, 110.

12. Holland, "Look to God and Live," *Ensign,* Nov. 1993, 14.

13. Bruce R. McConkie, "I Believe in Christ," *Hymns,* no. 134, v. 4. It is striking how often the hymns of the Restoration emphasize God's grace, mercy, and love. The following are but a sampling of lines from our hymns that emphasize this reality.

HOW FIRM A FOUNDATION

When through fiery trials thy pathway shall lie,
My grace, all sufficient, shall be thy supply.
The flame shall not hurt thee; I only design
Thy dross to consume and thy gold to refine.

The soul that on Jesus hath leaned for repose
I will not, I cannot, desert to his foes;
That soul, though all hell should endeavor to shake,
I'll never, no never, no never forsake!

(Robert Keen, "How Firm a Foundation,"
Hymns, no. 85, vv. 5, 7)

JESUS, THE VERY THOUGHT OF THEE

O hope of ev'ry contrite heart,
O joy of all the meek,
To those who fall, how kind thou art!
How good to those who seek!

(Bernard of Clairvaux, "Jesus, the Very
Thought of Thee," *Hymns,* no. 141, v. 3)

HOW GREAT THE WISDOM AND THE LOVE

How great, how glorious, how complete,
Redemption's grand design,
Where justice, love, and mercy meet
In harmony divine!
(Eliza R. Snow, "How Great the Wisdom and the Love," *Hymns,* no. 195, v. 6)

WHERE CAN I TURN FOR PEACE?

Constant he is and kind, Love without end.
(Emma Lou Thayne, "Where Can I Turn for Peace?" *Hymns,* no. 129, v. 3)

AS NOW WE TAKE THE SACRAMENT

We contemplate thy lasting grace,
Thy boundless charity;
To us the gift of life was giv'n
For all eternity.
(Lee Tom Perry, "As Now We Take the Sacrament," *Hymns,* no. 169, v. 1)

GOD LOVED US, SO HE SENT HIS SON

Oh, love effulgent, love divine!
What debt of gratitude is mine,
That in his off'ring I have part
And hold a place within his heart.
(Edward P. Kimball, "God Loved Us, So He Sent His Son," *Hymns,* no. 187, v. 3)

ROCK OF AGES

Not the labors of my hands
Can fill all thy law's demands;
Could my zeal no respite know,
Could my tears forever flow,

All for sin could not atone;
Thou must save, and thou alone.
(Augustus M. Toplady, "Rock of Ages," *Hymns,* no. 111, v. 2)

THE LORD IS MY LIGHT

The Lord is my light; the Lord is my strength.
I know in his might I'll conquer at length.
My weakness in mercy he covers with pow'r,
And, walking by faith, I am blest ev'ry hour.
(James Nicholson, "The Lord Is My Light," *Hymns,* no. 89, v. 3)

14. Smith, *Teachings,* 187. If God extends such mercy and love to us, we certainly are called to do the same for those with whom we interact each day. Joseph Smith taught: "But while one portion of the human race is judging and condemning the other without mercy, the Great Parent of the universe looks upon the whole of the human family with a fatherly care and paternal regard; He views them as His offspring, and without any of those contracted feelings that influence the children of men" (ibid., 218). And also this: "The nearer we get to our heavenly Father, the more we are disposed to look with compassion on perishing souls; we feel that we want to take them upon our shoulders, and cast their sins behind our backs. My talk is intended for all this society; if you would have God have mercy on you, have mercy on one another" (ibid., 241).

15. Samuel Medley, "I Know That My Redeemer Lives," *Hymns,* no. 136, v. 1.

16. Ibid., v. 2.

17. Ibid., v. 3.

18. See, for example, Nibley, *Ancient Documents and the Pearl of Great Price,* Lecture 14, p. 3; Lecture 19, p. 7; Lecture 22, p. 3; *Ancient State,* 316–17; "Passing of the Church," 143; *Approaching Zion,* 18–19, 30–31, 125–26, 463–64; *Brother Brigham Challenges the Saints,* 93; *Message of the Joseph Smith Papyri,* 258; *Mormonism and Early Christianity,* 16–17, 173–74; *Nibley on the Timely and the Timeless,* 53–54; *Old Testament and Related Studies,* 175–76, 177; *Prophetic Book of Mormon,* 462; *Since Cumorah,* 42; *Teachings of the Book of*

Mormon, semester 1, lecture 10, p. 11, and lecture 17, p. 4; semester 2, lecture 40, p. 9, and lecture 48, p. 14; semester 4, lecture 92, p. 72, and lecture 112, p. 280; *Temple and Cosmos,* xvii, 220; *World and the Prophets,* 105–6, 184–85; *Approach to the Book of Mormon,* 24, 485 n. 22.

19. Elder J. Richard Clarke of the Seventy taught: "The most damage to the Church is done by those who straddle the line, 'with one foot in the kingdom and the other in spiritual Babylon.' These people are playing on the Lord's and Satan's team . . . waiting to see which is winning before choosing sides" ("Be a Witness of God," *Church News,* 14 Apr. 1985, 21; see also Clarke, "Hold Up Your Light," *Ensign,* May 1985, 74). Likewise, of the willfully rebellious, the Prophet Joseph taught: "Our Heavenly Father is . . . more terrible to the workers of iniquity, more awful in the executions of His punishments, and more ready to detect every false way, than we are apt to suppose Him to be" (*Teachings,* 257).

20. *Captious* means "inclination to make petty criticisms or entrap or ensnare" (see *Merriam Webster's Collegiate Dictionary,* 11th ed.).

21. Clark, in Conference Report, Oct. 1953, 84.

22. Smith, *Teachings,* 239–40. Most of us project onto God our own personalities. We see God the way we see others. Thus, if we are prone to be judgmental and condemning of other people, we tend to see God as feeling that same way toward us. If, on the other hand, we're more inclined to be forgiving and merciful toward others, we tend to perceive God that way. Joseph Smith encouraged the Saints to see others with compassion, understanding, and forgiveness. As we do so, the Lord will pour out upon us His mercy in the form of compassion, understanding, and forgiveness. Quite literally, there is a correlation between the way we judge others and the way Christ will judge us.

23. We need to remember that Satan seeks to discourage us and dissuade us from righteousness every chance he gets. Feelings of discouragement never come from God; they are always of the devil. President Brigham Young once remarked: "Serve God according to the best knowledge you have, . . . and when the Devil comes along and says, 'You are not a very good Saint, you might enjoy greater blessings and more of the power of God, and have the vision of your mind opened, if you would live up to your privileges,' tell him to leave; that you have long ago forsaken his ranks and enlisted in the army of Jesus, who is your captain, and that you want no more of the Devil" (*Discourses,* 82).

24. Smith, *Teachings,* 255.

25. McConkie, "Probationary Test of Mortality," 12; see also Christofferson, "Justification and Sanctification," *Ensign,* June 2001, 25.

26. Used by permission.

27. Holland, "Look to God and Live," *Ensign*, Nov. 1993, 14–15.

28. Kimball, in *Journal of Discourses,* 4:222.

29. Hinckley, "Let Not Your Heart Be Troubled," in *Speeches of the Year, 1974,* 273.

Bibliography

Alexander, Thomas G. *Things in Heaven and Earth: The Life and Times of Wilford Woodruff, a Mormon Prophet.* Salt Lake City: Signature Books, 1991.

Ankerberg, John, and John Weldon. *Behind the Mask of Mormonism.* Eugene, Oreg.: Harvest House Publishers, 1996.

Bagnall, Roger S., and Bruce W. Frier. *The Demography of Roman Egypt.* New York: Cambridge University Press, 1994.

Barth, Markus. *Ephesians 1–3.* The Anchor Bible. New York: Doubleday, 1974.

Bednar, David A. "That We May Always Have His Spirit to Be with Us." *Ensign,* May 2006, 28–31.

Benson, Ezra Taft. *The Teachings of Ezra Taft Benson.* Salt Lake City: Bookcraft, 1998.

Bray, Gerald, ed. *1–2 Corinthians.* Ancient Christian Commentary on Scripture series. Downers Grove, Ill.: Inter Varsity Press, 1999.

———. *James, 1–2 Peter, 1–3 John, Jude.* Ancient Christian Commentary on Scripture series. Downers Grove, Ill.: Inter Varsity Press, 2000.

Brewster, Hoyt W., Jr. *Doctrine and Covenants Encyclopedia.* Salt Lake City: Bookcraft, 1988.

Brown, Raymond E. *The Death of the Messiah.* 2 vols. New York: Doubleday, 1994.

Brown, Raymond E., Joseph A. Fitzmyer, and Roland E. Murphy, eds. *The New Jerome Biblical Commentary.* Englewood Cliffs, N. J.: Prentice-Hall, 1990.

Bruce, F. F. *The Letter of Paul to the Romans: An Introduction and Commentary.*

The Tyndale New Testament Commentaries. Rev. ed. Grand Rapids, Mich.: Eerdmans, 1985.

Calhoun, Margie. *When Faith Writes the Story.* 2d ed. Salt Lake City: Bountiful Press, 1993.

Cannon, George Q. "Excerpts from Three Addresses by President Wilford Woodruff Regarding the Manifesto." In Doctrine and Covenants, 292.

Christofferson, D. Todd. "Justification and Sanctification." *Ensign,* June 2001, 18–25.

CIA. *World Fact Book.* Available online at https://www.cia.gov/library/publications/the-world-factbook/

Clark, J. Reuben, Jr. *Behold the Lamb of God.* Salt Lake City: Deseret Book, 1991.

———. In Conference Report. Oct. 1953, 83–84.

Clarke, J. Richard. "Be a Witness of God." *Church News,* 14 Apr. 1985, 21.

———. "'Hold Up Your Light.'" *Ensign,* May 1985, 73–75.

Coffin, William Sloane. "Sermon." Address delivered in Memorial Church, Stanford University, Palo Alto, California, 12 Mar. 2001.

Cole, R. Alan. *Galatians.* The Tyndale New Testament Commentaries. 2d ed. Grand Rapids, Mich.: Eerdmans, 1989.

Conybeare, W. H., and J. S. Howson. *The Life and Epistles of St. Paul.* Grand Rapids, Mich.: Eerdmans, 1968.

Davids, Peter H. *The First Epistle of Peter.* The New International Commentary on the New Testament. Grand Rapids, Mich.: Eerdmans, 1990.

Decker, Edward J. *Decker's Complete Handbook on Mormonism.* Eugene, Oreg.: Harvest House Publishers, 1995.

Draper, Richard D. *Opening the Seven Seals: The Visions of John the Revelator.* Salt Lake City: Deseret Book, 1991.

———, ed. *A Witness of Jesus Christ: The 1998 Sperry Symposium on the Old Testament.* Salt Lake City: Deseret Book, 1990.

Dummelow, J. R. *The One-Volume Bible Commentary.* New York: Macmillan, 1936.

Dunn, James D. G. *Romans 9–16.* Word Biblical Commentary. Dallas, Tex.: Word Books, 1988.

Ehat, Andrew F., and Lyndon W. Cook, comps. *The Words of Joseph Smith.* Provo, Utah: BYU Religious Studies Center, 1980.

Elliott, John H. *1 Peter.* The Anchor Bible. New York: Doubleday, 2000.

Ellis, Peter F. *Seven Pauline Letters.* Collegeville, Minn.: Liturgical Press, 1982.

Evans, Richard L. In Conference Report. Apr. 1955, 20–22.
Eyring, Henry B. "Gifts of the Spirit for Hard Times." *CES Fireside for Young Adults* [video]. Provo, Utah: Brigham Young University, 2006.
Faust, James E. In Conference Report. Apr. 1989, 39–43.
Fitzmyer, Joseph A. *Romans.* The Anchor Bible. New York: Doubleday, 1993.
Flinn, Michael W. *The European Demographic System, 1500–1820.* Brighton, England: Harvester Press Limited, 1981.
Foulkes, Francis. *Ephesians.* Rev. ed. The Tyndale New Testament Commentaries. Grand Rapids, Mich.: Eerdmans, 1997.
Gaebelein, Frank E., ed. *The Expositor's Bible Commentary.* 12 vols. Grand Rapids, Mich.: Zondervan, 1976–92.
Galbraith, Richard G. *Scriptural Teachings of the Prophet Joseph Smith.* Salt Lake City: Deseret Book, 1993.
Gaskill, Alonzo L. *The Lost Language of Symbolism: An Essential Guide for Recognizing and Interpreting Symbols of the Gospel.* Salt Lake City: Deseret Book, 2003.
Hafen, Bruce C., and Marie K. Hafen. *The Belonging Heart: The Atonement and Relationships with God and Family.* Salt Lake City: Deseret Book, 1994.
Hinckley, Bryant S. *Sermons and Missionary Services of Melvin Joseph Ballard.* Salt Lake City: Deseret Book, 1949.
Hinckley, Gordon B. "Let Not Your Heart Be Troubled." *Speeches of the Year, 1974.* Provo, Utah: Brigham Young University, 1975.
———. *Teachings of Gordon B. Hinckley.* Salt Lake City: Deseret Book, 1997.
Holland, Jeffrey R. *Christ and the New Covenant: The Messianic Message of the Book of Mormon.* Salt Lake City: Deseret Book, 1997.
———. "Look to God and Live." *Ensign,* Nov. 1993, 13–15.
"Hope for Parents of Wayward Children." *Ensign,* Sep. 2002, 11.
Huntington, Oliver B. "Sayings of Joseph Smith." *Young Woman's Journal* 2, no. 8 (May 1891): 366.
Hymns of The Church of Jesus Christ of Latter-day Saints. Salt Lake City: The Church of Jesus Christ of Latter-day Saints, 1985.
Jackson, Kent P. *From Apostasy to Restoration.* Salt Lake City: Deseret Book, 1996.
Jensen, Jay E. "Have I Received an Answer from the Spirit?" *Ensign,* Apr. 1989, 21–25.
Jensen, Margie Calhoun. *When Faith Writes the Story.* Salt Lake City: Bookcraft, 1973.

Johnston, Robert D. *Numbers in the Bible: God's Design in Biblical Numerology.* Grand Rapids, Mich.: Kregel, 1990.

Journal of Discourses. 26 vols. London: Latter-day Saints' Book Depot, 1854–86.

Kelly, J. N. D. *Early Christian Doctrines.* Rev. ed. San Francisco: Harper San Francisco, 1978.

Kimball, Spencer W. *Faith Precedes the Miracle.* Salt Lake City: Bookcraft, 1979.

———. *The Teachings of Spencer W. Kimball.* Ed. Edward L. Kimball. Salt Lake City: Bookcraft, 1982.

Largey, Dennis, et al., eds. *Book of Mormon Reference Companion.* Salt Lake City: Deseret Book, 2003.

Ludlow, Daniel H., ed. *Encyclopedia of Mormonism.* 4 vols. New York: Macmillan, 1992.

Lund, Anthon H. In Conference Report. Oct. 1903, 80–83.

Madsen, Truman G. *Joseph Smith the Prophet.* Salt Lake City: Bookcraft, 1989.

Manuscript History of Brigham Young, 1846–1847. Comp. Elden J. Watson. Salt Lake City: Smith Secretarial Service, 1971.

Marshall, I. Howard. *1 Peter.* The IVP New Testament Commentary. Downers Grove, Ill.: Inter Varsity Press, 1991.

Matthews, Robert J. "The Role of the House of Israel." Unpublished address to religious educators, Brigham Young University, 6 Mar. 1992.

Maxwell, Cory H., ed. *The Neal A. Maxwell Quote Book.* Salt Lake City: Bookcraft, 1997.

Maxwell, Neal A. *"But for a Small Moment."* Salt Lake City: Bookcraft, 1986.

———. *Deposition of a Disciple.* Salt Lake City: Bookcraft, 1976.

———. *Evening with a General Authority.* CES broadcast, Salt Lake City, 2 Feb. 2001.

———. *"For the Power Is in Them . . .": Mormon Musings.* Salt Lake City: Deseret Book, 1970.

———. "The Old Testament: Relevancy within Antiquity." In *1979 CES Old Testament Symposium.* Salt Lake City: The Church of Jesus Christ of Latter-day Saints, 1979.

———. *The Promise of Discipleship.* Salt Lake City: Deseret Book, 2001.

———. *A Wonderful Flood of Light.* Salt Lake City: Bookcraft, 1990.

McConkie, Bruce R. *Doctrinal New Testament Commentary.* 3 vols. Salt Lake City: Bookcraft, 1987–88.

———. "Funeral Address for Rebecca Adams." Address delivered 28 Oct. 1967. Copy in possession of the author.

———. "Jesus Christ and Him Crucified." In *Speeches of the Year, 1976*, Utah: Brigham Young University, 1977.

———. *The Millennial Messiah.* Salt Lake City: Deseret Book, 1982.

———. *Mormon Doctrine.* 2d ed. Salt Lake City: Bookcraft, 1979.

———. *The Mortal Messiah.* 4 vols. Salt Lake City: Deseret Book, 1980–81.

———. *A New Witness for the Articles of Faith.* Salt Lake City: Deseret Book, 1985.

———. "The Probationary Test of Mortality." Address delivered at Institute of Religion Devotional, Salt Lake City, 10 Jan. 1982.

———. *Sermons and Writings of Bruce R. McConkie.* Ed. Mark L. McConkie. Salt Lake City: Bookcraft, 1989.

———. "The Seven Deadly Heresies." In *Charge to Religious Educators.* 2d ed. Salt Lake City: The Church of Jesus Christ of Latter-day Saints, 1982; or in *Speeches of the Year, 1980.* Provo, Utah: Brigham Young University, 1981.

McConkie, Joseph Fielding. *Answers: Straightforward Answers to Tough Gospel Questions.* Salt Lake City: Deseret Book, 1998.

McConkie, Joseph Fielding, and Craig J. Ostler. *Revelations of the Restoration.* Salt Lake City: Deseret Book, 2000.

McConkie, Joseph Fielding, and Robert L. Millet. *Doctrinal Commentary on the Book of Mormon.* Vols. 1–3. Salt Lake City: Bookcraft, 1987–91.

McConkie, Joseph Fielding, Robert L. Millet, and Brent L. Top. *Doctrinal Commentary on the Book of Mormon.* Vol. 4. Salt Lake City: Bookcraft, 1992

Millet, Robert L. *Alive in Christ: The Miracle of Spiritual Rebirth.* Salt Lake City: Deseret Book, 1997.

———. *Within Reach.* Salt Lake City: Deseret Book, 1995.

Millet, Robert L., and Joseph Fielding McConkie. *The Life Beyond.* Salt Lake City: Bookcraft, 1987.

———. *Our Destiny: The Call and Election of the House of Israel.* Salt Lake City: Bookcraft, 1993.

Morris, Leon. *1 Corinthians.* Rev. ed. The Tyndale New Testament Commentaries. Grand Rapids, Mich.: Eerdmans, 1998.

Nelson, Russell M. "Doors of Death." *Ensign,* May 1992, 72–74.

———. "Perfection Pending." *Ensign,* Nov. 1995, 86–88.

———. "Tender Roots Need Strength." *Church News,* 14 Apr. 1985, 5.

Nibley, Hugh. *Ancient Documents and the Pearl of Great Price.* Ed. Robert Smith and Robert Smythe. Provo, Utah: FARMS, 1989.

———. *The Ancient State: The Rulers and the Ruled.* Ed. Donald W. Parry and Stephen D. Ricks. Provo, Utah: FARMS, 1991.

———. *An Approach to the Book of Mormon.* 3d ed. Provo, Utah: FARMS, 1988.

———. *Approaching Zion.* Ed. Don E. Norton. Provo, Utah: FARMS, 1989.

———. *Brother Brigham Challenges the Saints.* Ed. Don E. Norton and Shirley S. Ricks. Provo, Utah: FARMS, 1994.

———. *The Message of the Joseph Smith Papyri: An Egyptian Endowment.* Salt Lake City: Deseret Book, 1975.

———. *Mormonism and Early Christianity.* Ed. Todd M. Compton and Stephen D. Ricks. Provo, Utah: FARMS, 1987.

———. *Nibley on the Timely and the Timeless.* Provo, Utah: BYU Religious Studies Center, 1978.

———. *Old Testament and Related Studies.* Ed. John W. Welch, Gary P. Gillum, and Don E. Norton. Provo, Utah: FARMS, 1986.

———. "The Passing of the Church—Forty Variations on an Unpopular Theme." *BYU Studies* 16, no. 1 (Autumn 1975): 139–64.

———. *The Prophetic Book of Mormon.* Provo, Utah: FARMS, 1989.

———. *Since Cumorah.* 2d ed. Provo, Utah: FARMS, 1988.

———. *Teachings of the Book of Mormon.* Four semesters. Provo, Utah: FARMS, 1988–90.

———. *Temple and Cosmos: Beyond This Ignorant Present.* Ed. Don E. Norton. Provo, Utah: FARMS, 1992.

———. *The World and the Prophets.* 3d ed. Provo, Utah: FARMS, 1987.

Nicoll, W. Robertson. *The Expositor's Greek Testament.* 5 vols. Grand Rapids, Mich.: Eerdmans, 1983.

Oaks, Dallin H. "Preparation for the Second Coming." *Ensign,* May 2004, 7–10.

Ogden, D. Kelly, and Andrew C. Skinner. *The Four Gospels.* Vol. 1 of *Verse by Verse* series. Salt Lake City: Deseret Book, 2006.

Orr, William F., and James Arthur Walther. *1 Corinthians.* The Anchor Bible. New York: Doubleday, 1976.

Packer, Boyd K. "The Great Plan of Happiness." Address to CES Symposium, Brigham Young University, Provo, Utah, 10 Aug. 1993.

———. *The Holy Temple.* Salt Lake City: Bookcraft, 1980.

———. "Our Moral Environment." *Ensign,* May 1992, 66–68.

Parry, Jay A., and Donald W. Parry. *Understanding Death and the Resurrection.* Salt Lake City: Deseret Book, 2003.

———. *Understanding the Book of Revelation.* Salt Lake City: Deseret Book, 1998.

Powell, Mary Lucas. *Status and Health in Prehistory.* Washington, D.C.: Smithsonian Institution Press, 1988.

Reicke, Bo. *The Epistles of James, Peter, and Jude.* The Anchor Bible. New York: Doubleday, 1964.

Roberts, Alexander, and James Donaldson, eds. *Ante-Nicene Fathers.* 10 vols. Peabody, Mass.: Hendrickson Publishers, 1994.

Roberts, B. H. *The Gospel: An Exposition of Its First Principles.* 9th ed. Salt Lake City: Deseret Book, 1950.

———. *Outlines of Ecclesiastical History.* Salt Lake City: Deseret Book, 1979.

———, ed. *A Comprehensive History of The Church of Jesus Christ of Latter-day Saints.* 6 vols. Orem, Utah: Sonos, 1991.

Robinson, Stephen E. *Believing Christ: The Parable of the Bicycle and Other Good News.* Salt Lake City: Deseret Book, 1992.

Robinson, Stephen E., and H. Dean Garrett. *A Commentary on the Doctrine and Covenants.* 4 vols. Salt Lake City: Deseret Book, 2001–05.

Romney, Marion G. In Conference Report. Apr. 1944, 138–41.

———. "How Men Are Saved." *Ensign,* Nov. 1974, 38–40.

———. "The Worth of Souls." *Ensign,* Nov. 1978, 13–15.

Smith, Eldred G. In Conference Report. Apr. 1962, 65–67.

Smith, Hyrum, and Janne M. Sjodahl. *Doctrine and Covenants Commentary.* Rev. ed. Salt Lake City: Deseret Book, 1978.

Smith, James E. "Nephi's Descendants? Historical Demography and the Book of Mormon." A review of John C. Kunich, "Multiply Exceedingly: Book of Mormon Population Sizes." In *Review of Books on the Book of Mormon* 6, no. 1 (1994): 255–96.

Smith, John Henry. In Conference Report. Apr. 1908, 21–26.

Smith, Joseph. *History of The Church of Jesus Christ of Latter-day Saints.* Ed. B. H. Roberts. 2d ed. rev. 7 vols. Salt Lake City: Deseret Book, 1978.

———. *Joseph Smith.* In *Teachings of Presidents of the Church* series. Salt Lake City: IRI, 2007.

———. *Teachings of the Prophet Joseph Smith.* Sel. Joseph Fielding Smith. Salt Lake City: Deseret Book, 1976.

Smith, Joseph F. *Gospel Doctrine.* Salt Lake City: Deseret Book, 1999.

———. *Joseph F. Smith.* In *Teachings of Presidents of the Church* series. Salt Lake City: IRI, 1998.

Smith, Joseph Fielding. *Answers to Gospel Questions.* 5 vols. Salt Lake City: Deseret Book, 1993.

———. *Doctrines of Salvation.* 3 vols. in 1. Salt Lake City: Bookcraft, 1998.

———. *The Way to Perfection.* Salt Lake City: Genealogical Society of The Church of Jesus Christ of Latter-day Saints, 1931.

Smith, Mick. *The Book of Revelation: Plain, Pure, and Simple.* Salt Lake City: Bookcraft, 1998.

Stuy, Brian H., comp. *Collected Discourses Delivered by President Wilford Woodruff, His Two Counselors, the Twelve Apostles, and Others.* 5 vols. Burbank, Calif.: B.H.S. Publishing, 1987–92.

Talmage, James E. In Conference Report. Apr. 1915, 120–24.

———. *Jesus the Christ.* Salt Lake City: Deseret Book, 1983.

Taylor, John. *The Gospel Kingdom.* Ed. G. Homer Durham. Salt Lake City: Bookcraft, 1998.

Thatcher, Moses. "Mormon Polygamy and Christian Monogamy." *Contributor* 3, no. 6 (Mar. 1882): 162–65.

———. "Mormon Polygamy and Christian Monogamy." *Contributor* 3, no. 7 (Apr. 1882): 193–99.

Whitney, Orson F. In Conference Report, Apr. 1929, 109–15.

———. *Life of Heber C. Kimball.* Salt Lake City: Bookcraft, 1945.

———. *Saturday Night Thoughts.* Salt Lake City: Deseret News, 1921.

World Health Organization. *Human Development Reports.* Available online at http://www.who.int/en/

Woodbury, Charles. "This Person Has Accepted the Gospel." In "Faith Promoting Experiences of Patriarch Charles R. Woodbury." Manuscript. Utah State University Library, Logan, Utah.

Woodruff, Wilford. "Excerpts from Three Addresses by President Wilford Woodruff Regarding the Manifesto." In Doctrine and Covenants, 292.

Young, Brigham. *Discourses of Brigham Young.* Sel. John A. Widtsoe. Salt Lake City: Bookcraft, 1998.

Index